SO RUNS MY DREAM
The Story of Arthur and Keble Martin

*Stan
with my best wishes*

HILARY LEES

*Hilary
August 2004*

HALSGROVE

First published in Great Britain in 2001

Copyright © 2001 Hilary Lees

All rights reserved. No part of this publication may be reproduced, stored in a retrieval system, or transmitted in any form or by any means without the prior permission of the copyright holder.

British Library Cataloguing-in-Publication Data
A CIP record for this title is available from the British Library

ISBN 1 84114 138 0

HALSGROVE
PUBLISHING, MEDIA AND DISTRIBUTION

Halsgrove House
Lower Moor Way
Tiverton, Devon EX16 6SS
Tel: 01884 243242
Fax: 01884 243325
email: sales@halsgrove.com
website: www.halsgrove.com

Printed and bound in Great Britain by Bookcraft Ltd., Midsomer Norton.

Whilst every care has been taken to ensure the accuracy of the information contained in this book, the author disclaims responsibility for any mistakes which may have inadvertently been included.

CONTENTS

ACKNOWLEDGEMENTS	4
SO RUNS MY DREAM	5
GROWING UP	11
THE DARTMOOR DIARIES	19
THE PRE-WAR YEARS	25
SANDHURST	35
HACCOMBE AND COFFINSWELL	42
COLOUR PLATES	49
THE DREAM CHURCH	57
TWO CHURCHES	69
LATER YEARS	75
THE FLORA	81
PUBLICATION	85
APPENDIX: *The Dartmoor Diaries*	93
BIBLIOGRAPHY	141
INDEX	142

FOR EDWARD AND SOPHIE
the next generation

ACKNOWLEDGEMENTS

I would like to thank all those people whose help and encouragement have made this book possible, especially:
Rev. Paul Ensor
Roger Halliday, Duchy of Cornwall
Rev. Jim Jelley
Rev. Tim and Moira Leach
Father John Potter
Jock Stanier
Ann and Malcolm Stocker
Dr P. J. Thwaites, Sandhurst Collection

From the Martin family:
Stephanie and John Brownbridge
Dot Carter
Lisette Whitney
and in particular Richard Martin
and my mother Audrey Harbord

SO RUNS MY DREAM

This is the story of a dream. Not the dream that evaporates on waking, but one that persists through years of planning and fund-raising until finally the dream becomes the tangible bricks and mortar of a modern church. This is the unique and remarkable story of two brothers and their realisation of this dream; of the little church of Milber, man's witness to the power and glory of God.

In March 1931 Keble Martin, the busy Rector of the combined parishes of Haccombe and Coffinswell with Milber, Devon, woke up one morning with the distinct recollection of a dream. At that time Milber had no church; the previous year a wooden mission room had been built for the combined purposes of church and social gatherings, leaving the parish in considerable debt. Of the dream Keble recollects:

> I was preaching in a new church building from the chancel step. The church was filled with people, and was of a curious pattern. The altar stood in a round stone apse behind me. There were three diverging naves in front of me, one unfinished..... When the congregation had left I walked out by the central nave, and could see through the arches into the lateral nave.

It was to be 32 years before the completion of St Luke's, Milber, also known affectionately as the Dream Church. Today the church, with its unorthodox design and informal atmosphere, stands as a symbol of the power of Keble Martin's vision, and the exceptional insight and talent of the architect, his brother Arthur Campbell Martin. Much later, at the age of 88, Keble Martin became a household name with the publication of *The Concise British Flora in Colour*, a collection of paintings that were his life's work. The two brothers, the botanist and the architect have between them left a legacy that will endure for generations.

Arthur and Keble Martin were fifth and sixth respectively in a large Victorian family of nine children. Their father was Charles Martin, Warden (headmaster) of Radley and then Rector of Dartington, Devon. Their mother was Dora Moberley, one of the 15 children of George Moberley, headmaster of Winchester for 31 years and later

Rev. Charles Martin, Warden of Radley College, 1870-1879.

Bishop of Salisbury. From Keble Martin's autobiography, *Over The Hills* there is a fond recollection of how this came about:

> My father used to go by horse coach from South Devon to Winchester and at Winchester College he became in due course Prefect of Hall, ie. Head Boy, and he married Dora Moberley, a younger daughter of George Moberly the Headmaster of Winchester. Thus the Head Boy married the headmaster's daughter, but had to wait till he was 29 before he could afford to marry. The wedding took place on Holy Cross Day, 14 September 1869 at St Mary's, Brighstone, on the Isle of Wight, because for a short period her father, George Moberly, was Rector of Brighstone between his time at Winchester and the Bishopric of Salisbury. So when my mother was collecting her wedding trousseau, her father was getting ready his Episcopal robes. He was consecrated Bishop that autumn.

Dora Martin had herself had a similar upbringing to that of her husband, and already knew all there was to know about the life of a clergy wife. Her father, Bishop George Moberly, was a close friend of John Keble, a leading member of the Oxford Movement. During the years when he had been Headmaster of Winchester the family had spent the school holidays at Field House in Hursley, not far from Winchester, where John Keble was Rector. The two families saw a great deal of one another, and the Moberly children often went to play at the Rectory.

After what had been a critical moment in the history of the Church of England the two men would have had much to discuss. One of Dora's sisters, Catherine, writes in *Dulce Domum* that her father, 'while no disciple of Mr Keble's, yet he did most fully appreciate the newly recovered hold on Church doctrine won for England by the Oxford Movement.'[1] She goes on to say:

> It is difficult to overestimate the richness, fullness and variety of living interests which they brought into the lives of one another. It is probable that each one had many more personally like-minded friends – friends corresponded with constantly and met occasionally – but for these three (the novelist Charlotte Yonge was often in the party) there was the exceedingly close bond of neighbourliness. It was an actual daily intercourse which made the tie so binding. On Wednesdays and Fridays, after the service, Mr Keble and Doctor Moberly frequently spent the rest of the morning walking up and down the country road in uninterrupted conversation: even if not agreed on all points, they must have taken a great amount of counsel on many subjects from one another during these walks.

---

[1] The Oxford Movement, so called because it was centred on Oxford University, was led by J. H. Newman, Richard Hurrell Froude, John Keble and Edward Pusey, Canon of Christ Church, Oxford. Its aim was to bring about a return within the Church of England to the high-church ideals of the seventeenth century. For many years the Church of Rome had monopolised the concept of Catholicism, and the term 'catholic' had come to mean exclusively Roman Catholics. Keble's sermon 'National Apostasy' on July 14th 1833 marked the beginning of the Oxford Movement. It demonstrated his strong and uncompromising conviction that the Church's divine right was derived from direct apostolic descent from Christ himself. The group published 90 Tracts of the Times and produced a revival of the Anglican theology of the seventeenth century. Although Keble led a quiet and contemplative life at Hursley, he was the inspiration behind the movement. Keble College, Oxford, was founded in his memory in 1869.

Much of the correspondence between the two families is recorded in *Dulce Domum*, and Catherine herself says:

> It was no restful position to be Mr Keble's next door neighbour for 30 years, and especially such years for the Church of England as from 1836 to 1866, for every phase of Church politics was watched, discussed, and prayed over at Hursley. Mr Keble took up every point of State policy which affected the Church and of religious controversy with keen anxiety.

It is easy to speculate how deeply Dora Moberly and her brothers and sisters would have been affected by the central importance of the Church in their parents' lives, and how, having herself married a scholar and churchman, this influence would have been carried through to her own children. There was later to be another small link with the Keble family: one of Keble Martin's godparents was Philip Champernowne, a cousin on Charles Martin's side, whose mother was a niece of John Keble. The Champernownes lived at Dartington Hall, where Charles Martin was to become Rector.

Dora Moberly's sister, Frances was to marry Rev. William Awdry, another prolific family of cousins that the Martin family knew all their lives. Theirs was the generation that grew up in the late Victorian period of rigid values and social divides. They were to be decimated by the Great War, and those that survived would see another generation of young men wasted in a second horrendous conflict.

The opening words of Keble Martin's autobiography read: 'The character of a native flower is very dependent on the kind of seed from which it has grown, and upon the soil in which it is rooted. Here then is the seed and the soil.'

The earliest recorded ancestor of the Martin family was William Martin (1584-1654) who was three times Mayor of Evesham and a Justice of the Peace. His only surviving son Thomas (1619-1679) was also twice Mayor and a Justice of the Peace, described on his memorial as 'a terrour to evill doers and a praise to them that did well.' His son William (1654-1685) continued the civic tradition and in the next generation his son Thomas (1680-1675) who was only 14 years old when William died at the age of 41, was the first member of the family to be associated with the banking business which later became Martin's Bank in Lombard Street in the City of London. Martin's Bank continued to flourish in the hands of successive generations of the Martin family for nearly 300 years until it was taken over by Barclays in 1968.

Two generations later two brothers both took livings in Devon and established what became known affectionately as the 'Devonshire Martins'. The elder, George, was Vicar of Harberton and Chancellor of Exeter Diocese. His brother, William, was Vicar of Staverton, Devon, and had married Jane Champernowne, whose family had lived at Dartington Hall since the sixteenth century. They had a family of eight boys and five girls, all born and baptised at Staverton between 1829 and 1850. Charles Martin was the fifth son.

Both the Martin and the Moberly families came from a strong Christian tradition. George Moberly and his wife Mary Anne had 15 children, all of whom lived beyond childhood and were brought up in the rarefied and academic atmosphere of the precincts of Winchester College. Dora Frances, born in 1841 was the sixth child and fourth daughter and was a talented watercolour artist.

Dora and Charles Martin with Edith at Radley, 1870.

Charles and Dora had nine children, and later generations of the family could recite the names by rote: Edith, Dora, Charlie, Jack, Arthur, Keble, Nellie, Mollie, Dick.

Their first daughter, Edith was born in 1869 at Harrow, where Charles had accepted a mastership, but the subsequent six children, including Arthur and Keble, were all born at Radley. According to family folklore, Dora was strongly advised by her doctor to 'have a rest' after the first six of her children, but shows no sign of having done so.

Charles was appointed Warden of Radley in 1870, at a time when the school was making a difficult adjustment from the mid-Victorian to the 'modern' outlook. Charles was able to increase the number of pupils and achieve satisfactory academic standards,

The family at Wood Norton, 1880.

but he was not a natural disciplinarian, and this led to a number of clashes with other members of staff and with disruptive groups of pupils. His greatest pleasure was in preparing pupils for Confirmation in the chapel. In 1879 he resigned, and in complete contrast accepted the living of the rural parish of Wood Norton in Norfolk. (Colour Plate 1)

It must have been a difficult move; Dora was pregnant at the time, and because of the poor condition of the rectory the family had to live in temporary accommodation at Twyford, nearby. The two churches in Charles' care, one at Wood Norton and the other at Swanton Novers, were both in need of repair, and during Charles' incumbency major restoration work was carried out on both churches. It was in Norfolk that the last two of their children, Mary Katherine (Mollie) and Richard (Dick) were born.

Meanwhile Charles gave his attention to improvements to the Rectory, for which he obtained a mortgage of £375 from Queen Anne's Bounty in March 1880. The repairs included alterations to the ground floor and the bedrooms as well as the installation of a water closet to replace the privy. The water from the well contained 'the oxidised products of sewage in very large proportion'. They were obliged to sink a new well some distance from the house, and until the water could be piped it was presumably carried by hand in sufficient quantities to meet the needs of a large family.

In the autumn of 1883 the family moved to Poulshot, Wiltshire, bringing them back into the Diocese of Salisbury, where Dora's father, George Moberly was by then Bishop. The two boys, Arthur and Keble were then eight and six respectively and their brother

Jack was nine. Keble remembers an occasion soon after their return to Poulshot when he and his father had gone into Devizes in the wagonette. Charles passed the reins to Keble with instructions to 'hold them tight, hold them tight,' while he went into the bank. Keble, only six years old, was so keen to comply that he tugged at the reins as hard as he could. The horse obediently backed the cart up on to the pavement, and towards the windows of the bank, but fortunately Charles reappeared just in time to rescue the situation.

The whole family would occasionally go by train to visit Bishop Moberly at Salisbury, having got up at six o'clock in the morning to take the wagonette to Devizes station. The train journey caused great excitement among the younger children. In the Close at Salisbury they were impressed by the sheer magnificence of the Cathedral in its superb setting, and Arthur was to remember all his life his first impressions of the tall pointing finger of the spire and the great columns and arches of the interior. One can imagine the young family in favoured pews drinking in the ritual, the colour and the music.

They were fascinated but undaunted by the grandeur of the Bishop's Palace, where the candelabras were lit with a candle on a long holder, and where there was a secret door in the bookcase of the Bishop's study.

At Poulshot the three boys, close in age, enjoyed the freedom of the large Rectory garden. Their uncle Edward Moberly, who used to come and give their sisters violin lessons, supplied the boys with everything required for collecting butterflies and moths: nets, setting boards and even boxes for rearing them from caterpillars. He also taught them how to collect and store birds' eggs and how to make wooden cabinets for displaying insects. He also taught them the elements of archery, with such success that one day they found that one of their arrows had hit a pig; they then had the problem of catching it before they could remove the arrow from the thick hide. Fortunately the pig was none the worse for being used inadvertently for target practice.

Much of this activity, normal to small boys in the late nineteenth century, and which did so much to increase the brothers' interest and knowledge of birds and flowers, was in later generations to become unacceptable. Post-war social changes due largely to urban development and new farming techniques meant that many of the butterflies and flowers which the children treated so lightly were to become endangered species. However all the members of the Martin family developed a keen interest in natural history which they pursued on the moors and rivers of Devon, and later on holidays and in leisure time.

It was evidently a happy, carefree childhood for the Martin family. Dora, Keble and Arthur had all inherited their mother's artistic talent and the children were all able to enjoy the freedom of a large garden and to occupy themselves happily.

The Martin children were growing up at a time when the class system was approaching its peak, and when a third of the country's population lived below subsistence level. It is to the credit of Charles and Dora Martin that they raised their family with a strong sense of Christian duty and an awareness of their own good fortune when so many were struggling to survive.

GROWING UP

In his autobiography *Over The Hills* Keble Martin's chapter on the boys' school days starts with a modest understatement:

> We were just ordinary average boys like thousands of others, learning to be humble, none of us distinguished as scholars or athletes.

When they were small the Martin children were taught by a governess, as was usual towards the end of the nineteenth century. At the age of ten Arthur was said by his sisters to be 'a bother to Mother, a tease to Billy (Keble) and a plague to us'. The family were still living at Poulshot, and he was packed off to boarding school at Eton House, Aldeburgh, Suffolk, to be joined by Keble a year later. Keble writes:

> This was the summer of 1887 and Queen Victoria's first Jubilee. In the short hours of darkness the windows in the town were illuminated with candles arranged in the pattern of V.R. The shingle came up at that time to the walls of the Town Hall. And the bonfire was made on the shingle to the north of the town.

As a budding botanist even at that tender age he always said that the bonfire was built on a precious clump of sea-pea; however walks along the coast gave the boys their first introduction to an abundance of seaside flowers.

A year later Keble went to a school at Lyme Regis, where he seems to have been on the receiving end of the cane on numerous occasions. He remembers one momentous event when he and a couple of other boys had 'flu, there was a fire further down the street and they got out of bed to watch what was going on. Bishop John Wordsworth was staying in a building opposite where the fire was, and the boys circulated a story that the Bishop had joined the firefighters with a bucket and had gone too close to the fire, having to be pulled out by his heels.

The following year he was moved again, to Waynefleet School in Bristol, where Arthur joined him. Reading between the lines, perhaps his interest in botany exceeded his desire for a formal education. Finally, however, in 1891, the year that the family moved to Dartington, he went to Marlborough; there the Natural History Society together with the attractions of Savernake Forest cemented what was to be his life-long passion for botany.

Meanwhile, Arthur, a year previously, had moved on to Winchester, where his academic record seems to have been singularly undistinguished. He did not manage to get into the sixth form, but left from the form below it. A silver cup, still in the family, records that he won the double fives competition in 1893 for Southgate House.

During the holidays the brothers enjoyed many happy days together in the woods of the Dart valley. Keble remembers large numbers of red squirrels; the grey squirrel had not yet arrived.

There were such a lot of red squirrels. We enjoyed seeing them, running up the tree in jerks and stopping to cough at us. One day I peeped into a chaffinch's nest in a laurel bush, moss and lichen lined with hair. There was one egg, then I saw a squirrel coming across the wood, finally running down a stem and on to the laurel, straight to the chaffinch's nest (he knew it was there), taking it quickly in his mouth, tipping the egg out right in front of my nose, then taking the nest up the stem and back across the wood to the dray in the top of a tall holly for his mate to line the dray with.

The Martins were a large, happy family brought up in a strong Christian tradition. The oldest, Edith, was tall and thin, and could be bossy and alarming, taking her responsibilities as the oldest seriously. She left home early to earn her living as a court dressmaker, and her home in London was a convenient pied-a-terre for her brothers and sisters when they had to be in London on business or were passing through. Both Arthur and Keble stayed there on their way to war service in France.

Dora is described as a gentle saint; she had inherited her mother's gift as a talented watercolour artist, and played the violin cello. On several occasions she kept house for her relatives, including Keble. For about nine years when the need arose she looked after her uncle Walter Moberly when he was Vicar of Sydenham.

Charlie, the eldest of the brothers, was a fruit farmer for Lord Sudeley at Toddington in Gloucestershire. He is said to have had a bald head and a deep laugh loud enough to

Dartington Parsonage at the end of the nineteenth century.

lift the rafters of his barn. He was responsible for the planting of more than a thousand acres of fruit trees high in the Cotswolds and was much sought after in an advisory capacity. In later years Keble and his wife used to visit him to explore the flora of the Cotswold beech woods and the oolite soil.

The next brother, Jack, left Oxford to go into a shipbuilding company in Glasgow, but 'he was so shocked by his fellow workers that after a year there he gave it up'. He offered himself for ordination and attended Cuddesdon Theological College. He was a kindly, gentle man and because he was curate at Ottery St Mary and subsequently had livings at Simonsbath and Dartington, he was dubbed the 'Parson of Exmoor'.

The two younger sisters, Nellie and Katharine were both musical, and during the years at Poulshot were taught by their uncle Edward Moberly, who was conductor of the Avon Vale orchestra. At Dartington they played the piano and violin and together with Dora and friends formed the 'family orchestra' and entertained the family in the winter evenings. They also played with the Exeter Cathedral Orchestra and took music pupils for lessons. In due course both became Licentiates of the Royal Academy of Music.

None of the girls ever married, and family gossip has it that no one was felt to be good enough for them. If there were male students staying in the house, as sometimes happened, the girls were packed off to stay with relatives in case temptation loomed.

The youngest brother, Dick, trained as an engineer at the Central Technical College. He went to South West Africa to survey the Angola Railway for the Portuguese Government, living only in tents in a dry desert area among dangerous snakes and lions. He returned with a butterfly collection which he and Keble took to the Natural History Collection. Later he was for a long time Chief Engineer to the South India Railway, returning finally to Exmouth.

Charles Martin's predecessor at Dartington was his uncle Richard Champernowne, who had married Elizabeth, daughter of Thomas Keble of Bisley, Gloucestershire. The Champernowne family had lived at Dartington Hall since the reign of Queen Elizabeth I, a period of some 350 years. They were cousins of the Martins, both being descended from Arthur Champernowne and his wife Louisa, who died in 1870 at the age of 92. When Richard Champernowne died in 1890 his great-nephew Arthur Melville Champernowne offered the living to Charles Martin.

The children of the two families were remarkably similar in age: the Champernowne children of six boys and four girls were all born between 1871 and 1885. The Martin's five boys and four girls were born between 1870 and 1885; it is not surprising that the children grew up with fond and happy memories of their years at Dartington. Keble has an entertaining recollection from those boyhood years:

> The crows were rascals. The poultry at Dartington had a free run, and generally did well on it, but they sometimes made a nest on the hedge-bank of a near orchard. A crow would sit on an apple tree and wait till the hen came off cackling with joy over another egg laid. The crow popped down, drove his bill through the egg, and so carried it to his nest in a big spruce fir in the neighbouring wood to feed his family. The ground below this nest was thickly strewn with the eggshells.

Dartington Hall is recorded in the Domesday Book, but the whole complex including the Parsonage as it now stands was rebuilt in 1380-1400 by John Holand, Duke of Exeter,

Dartington Parsonage as it is today.

half-brother to Richard II. His crest, a white hart on a red rose, is still to be found in the roof of the porch in the main tower of the Hall.

The Parsonage was built for the Rectors of Dartington parish, and was a family home for 500 years until the Elmhirst family bought it in 1925. They lived there themselves while restoration work was carried out on Dartington Hall, which was to become a centre for 'education and the Arts as essential to a rich and creative life'. Since then the Parsonage has been a part of the Dartington Hall Trust, providing residential courses in 'New World' studies. It was known as The Old Postern for some years until it was renamed Schumacher College in 1991 after E. F. Schumacher, the author of *Small is Beautiful*.

The original church of St Mary's, Dartington, with the exception of the tower, had been demolished in 1878, and the materials used to build a new church nearer the main road in the same Perpendicular style and the same dimensions. Perhaps the proximity of the church bells to the private rooms of the Champernownes caused some inconvenience. The reredos of the new church was designed by Arthur in 1906; the leaflet notes that it was paid for by public subscription, but there is no mention of the designer.

Dartington Parsonage is situated at the bottom of the road leading to the Hall and within easy reach of St Mary's Church. There was originally a walled forecourt, of which all that remains is the length of wall at the east end of the building, still with its original doorway. From the same period the central part of the building survives, including the castellated porch with a room above and the rooms to the east. To the right of the porch there was at one time a room on the upper floor, but at some point this was removed so that the dining room, on the right of the front door went right up

GROWING UP

The reredos, Dartington Church, designed by Arthur Martin.

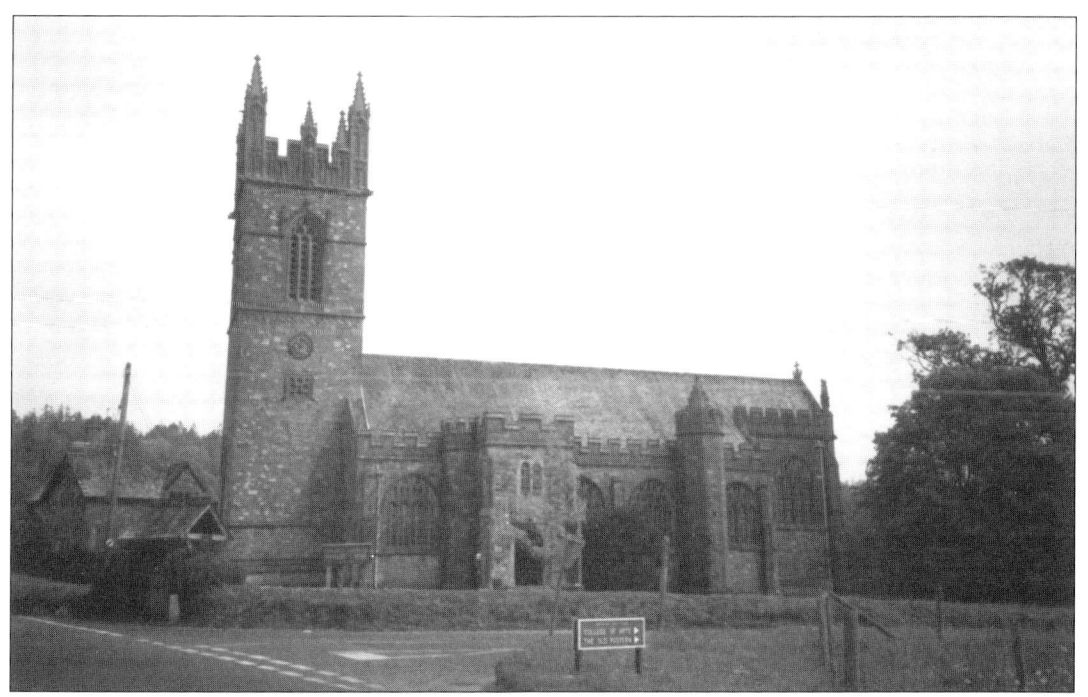

Dartington Church, spiritual home of the 'Devonshire' Martins.

to the roof, with a so-called minstrels' gallery providing access to the small bedroom over the porch. It is described by the youngest son, Dick, in his autobiography:

> On entering the front door my father's study, surrounded by bookshelves, was on the left and the dining room was on the right. The later was a large room stretching up to the curved rafters of the roof, and had a gallery at the near end. For some years there was a church organ at the far end of the room, yet on rare occasions we sat down as many as sixteen to a meal. The gallery, which was sometimes called 'The Minstrels' Gallery' led to a bedroom over the porch, and how eerie it could seem when after dark, one walked along the gallery to this little bedroom by the light of a guttering candle, while a few flickering flames in the large dining room fireplace made shadows of unearthly shape dance on the curved ceiling above one's head.

In 1799 Robert Froude rebuilt the whole of the west wing, planted shrubs and drained the pond. At some stage grottoes and a butter-well were built in the Parsonage copse, and remains of these can still be seen.

In about 1860 William White carried out major works which were reported in the *Ecclesiologist* of 1861:

> Mr White has admirably restored and rearranged the Rectory at Dartington, a triangular building with ancient remains on the south and east fronts; a roofed hall which had been cut into two heights for bedrooms was restored, the modern windows being replaced with others of good design. The east front has been entirely rebuilt, and the whole appearance of the house greatly improved. The central hall will have a gallery, the woodwork of which is excellently designed; the same may be said of the details throughout.

A plan of the house from 1935 shows it to have been a large house with a sizeable servants' wing and as many as 13 bedrooms. In the 1891 census return the persons in the house were:

Charles Martin	aged 50
Dora his wife	aged 49
Edith	aged 20
Dora	aged 19
Charles	aged 18
John	aged 16
Arthur	aged 15
Margaret	aged 11
Katherine	aged 10
Richard	aged 9

Keble is not mentioned and was evidently away at the time. Also in the census are a Mr James Pearce, his wife and four children. The parents' occupations are given as gardener and domestic servant. The birthplace of James and the children is given as Poulshot, so evidently this family came with the Martins from the previous parish.

GROWING UP

The family at Dartington in 1893. Front row: *Charles, Mother, Father, Eleanor.*
Back row from left: *John, Katherine, Edith, Keble, Dora, Dick, Arthur.*

In addition there would have been daily staff coming in from the village, as was customary at the time.

Dartington Parsonage and its surrounding countryside left a lasting memory with the children of the family as the spiritual centre of the 'Devonshire Martins'. It was their home during the formative years of adolescence and early adulthood when they were still free of responsibilities. Together with their Champernowne cousins at the Hall they enjoyed walking, fishing and birdwatching and playing tennis. Surely Arthur had Dartington in mind when he was later to write in his book *The Small House*:

> If we think how the sight or thought of some feature in the home brings back old associations and the vivid recollection of incidents we had forgotten, we see how close is the connection between the features of the design and the family life. In our first conception of the building, while discussing the details of the various portions, we must remember that every nook and corner in the house and every turn in the garden path is destined to be a matter of history as we, or our children look back in after-years; and it may well be they will form the children's first recollections, and remain forever the type with which they compare all other houses.

Brought up in this secure and academic atmosphere, the boys had a happy childhood with plenty of freedom. They were all keen botanists and bird-watchers, an interest

Five years later. Back row from left: *Dick, Edith, Charles, Eleanor.*
Middle row: *Keble, Mother, Jack, Father, Arthur.* Front row: *Dora and Katherine.*

which was to stay with them all their lives. The two brothers were very different: Arthur had a quiet sense of humour and a quick tongue; it was always said of him that he hardly said a word until he was three. Then, when he was at a children's party one day he pointed to the table and said with perfect diction: 'I'll have some of that, and some of that, and some of that, and then I'll have a glass of water to wash it down.'

In a family photograph taken in the Parsonage grounds in 1898 the bearded Charles sits in the middle of his family. Arthur is shown as a good-looking, smartly dressed young man sitting cross-legged, reclining in a chair and looking away from the family group as though bored with the proceedings. Keble also seems to have his eye on a distant horizon, while Dora and her mother are enjoying some private joke.

There is no doubt that the happy years at Dartington did much to equip the children for later life. For Arthur and Keble it was to shape their future lives and to stand them in good stead during the difficult years ahead.

Charles Martin was to stay at Dartington until he died in 1910. The family was then obliged to leave the Rectory and moved to Ottery St Mary, where Jack was curate; he was later Rector of Dartington like his father.

Charles was buried in the churchyard at Dartington; his memorial records that he was born on the 17th October 1840 and died on 23rd February 1910. He had been Rector of Dartington for 19 years. The adjacent memorial records the death of his wife Dora Martin, born on the 18th December 1841 and died on the 24th January 1926.

THE DARTMOOR DIARIES

From the years 1905-1910 Arthur and Keble, together with friends and relations enjoyed short camping holidays on Dartmoor. At the time the holidays began, the ages of the Martin family ranged from 24 to 32, and those of the Champernownes from 20 to 34. Regular members of the camp were the three Martin brothers, Jack, Arthur and Keble; their cousins from Dartington Hall, Gilbert and Bob Champernowne, another cousin William Martin, known as Willy and Arthur Medlicott, architect and friend of Arthur.

For the first six years an illustrated diary recording the holidays was kept by Arthur, with maps and detailed housekeeping accounts; also all sorts of anecdotal detail, including graphic accounts of many of the disasters which overtook them. It is written with Arthur's dry humour; his line drawings demonstrate with architectural precision some of the mishaps which befell them, such as a frog occupying Jack's clerical collar at 4.30 am one morning, and the collapse of the kitchen tent in a storm.

The camps usually took place in late July on an area of Dartmoor close to Puppers Hill, about 1,400 feet above sea level. The distance is recorded as 'two hours up from the Parsonage (Dartington) by bicycle and one and a quarter hours down; two hours walk from Buckfastleigh and one and three-quarter hours down'. The camp site was close to the Warren stream, a tributary of the River Avon, which each year they blocked with stones to provide a bathing pool and dairy, as well as supplying them with a regular source of trout. Their only immediate link with the outside world was Warren House, a farm half a mile away where the keeper, or warrener and his wife supplied them with milk and bread and the occasional rabbit pie. The two parsons in the party, Jack and Keble, were able to reciprocate by christening the youngest child of the family on behalf of the Vicar of Lydford; the baptism had to be entered in the church register 21 miles away as the crow flies. The Warrener's three children walked five miles a day each way across the moor to school at Holne, sometimes in dense cloud.

The campers took two tents, one a regulation bell-tent, bought second-hand for 35s. 6d. from M. Tope of Plymouth, the second 'a little calico tent manufactured at home and used as our kitchen'. They had two paraffin stoves for cooking, but they were a mixed blessing 'owing perhaps to the subtle drafts of the open moor, they took an hour to bring a saucepan and forty minutes to bring a kettle to the boil'. Later they built a peat fire in a hollow, on which they then did most of the cooking. The men slept in the bell tent with their feet meeting at the central pole like the spokes of a wheel.

The holidays seem to have been a constant battle against the weather. On several occasions they had to dig trenches round the tents to divert the rain, and once during the 1905 camp the back was blown out of the kitchen tent and the bell tent was leaning dangerously. The event is graphically illustrated by Arthur's line drawings. Finally the camp was defeated by the weather, and the 'home office' at the Parsonage despatched the horse and cart to bring the sodden campers home.

Map showing position of Warren House and the chapel.

∽ THE DIARIES ∼

Camp photos.

In subsequent years the members of the party varied but the routine was the same. Arthur's record of the provisions consumed by a party of seven persons during the 1906 camp makes interesting reading:

Daily:	5 lbs bread; 3½ pints of milk
Weekly:	2 beef steak pies; 2 rabbit pies; 1 leg of mutton 11 lbs
	1 Ham (2 halves); 1 English tongue; 4lbs bacon (5 times)
	5 lbs plain cake; 1 lb cheese; 1½lbs butter (not v good)
	1 doz hard boiled eggs; 20 fresh eggs; 1lb Devon cream
	Dartmoor trout
Groceries:	2½ large packets Quaker oats; ½lb cornflower
	1½lbs tea; 2 lbs loaf sugar; 1lb gran sugar (ran out);
	½lb brown sugar; 12 lbs jam (too much alike); 2lbs wortleberries
	lumps of dripping; tin of salt; some mustard; a little pepper

Many of the party were competent fishermen (it was said that Arthur could land a fly in a teacup at 50 yards) and Dartmoor trout and unlimited rabbits formed a substantial part of their diet. Sometimes they entertained visitors, usually the ladies from the Parsonage and the Hall, who were brought by carriage as far as Heyford and walked from there. Before leaving they were usually asked politely if they would be so kind as to wash up.

The minor mishaps that were inevitable provided much amusement. On one occasion Medlicott dropped the soap in the bathing pool and in spite of all his efforts was unable to retrieve it. It lay there, an unlikely-looking stone, for the fish to make of it what they could. Another day, one of the campers was washing broad beans by the stream in a cracked bowl when it broke, sending all the beans into the water. With great presence of mind he ran downstream to the next waterfall and was able to catch every bean as it arrived.

Keble comes across as extremely preoccupied, a condition described more recently by his daughter as 'not on this planet'. He was always a late starter, and having got going would frequently get lost, turning up late bearing large collections of 'weeds and things'. However what the family called his 'botanising' was very productive; the second year he informed the assembled company 'in an almost distressed tone of voice' that his bed was made of *Potentilla tormentilla*, *Hyloconimum squarrosum* and *Agrostis alba*, which he explained were a flower, a moss and a grass respectively. There is no suggestion that his botanical bed was not comfortable. The following year there was great excitement when he found his first specimen of *Corydalis*; this was identified in a wood below Sharp Tor which inevitably became known as 'Keble's Wood'.

At the end of the diary for the 1907 camp is a list of suggestions for the following year:

That the frying pan should not have any large holes in it.
That there should be a plum pudding.
That breakfast cups hold more than tea cups.
That we should borrow a quart can for carrying milk.
That we should take enough matches and cocoa, also saucepan brush and hone.

THE DIARIES

The 1908 camp starts with a list of those attending and, for some reason, their weights. Keble was so late that he was not weighed. Supper the first evening consisted of 'mutton, hot potatoes and peas, followed by an excellent plum pudding, not forgetting the hot cocoa before turning in'. Evidently the list of suggestions had borne fruit. It was another very wet camp, and Arthur's illustrations show an improvised larder on a long stick. His love of birds is apparent all the way through the diaries, and in the following year, 1909, he records meadow pipits and wheatears as well as snipe, plover and missel thrushes. It was a hot year, and the campers made a dairy in the stream in which milk, cream and butter could be kept, 'and in which blancmanges and other delicacies' (brought by the visiting ladies) could be kept cool. Warren House seems to have been temporarily empty, and they were obliged to go to Heyford Farm for supplies. One evening Jack and Keble were returning from the farm with bread when Keble suddenly dropped his load to examine a plant. He had found a new variety of moss.

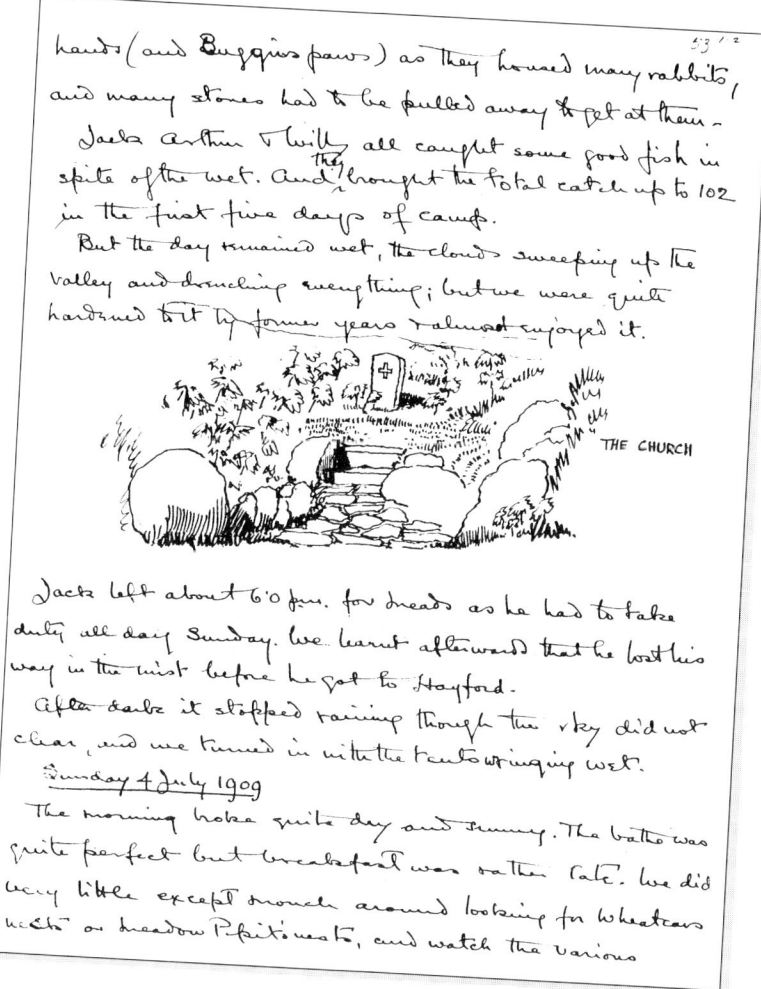

A page from the diaries with Arthur's sketch of the chapel.

It was during this camp in 1909 that they created a church in a hollow across the stream. They paved the floor roughly with slabs, building three steps up to a small grass terrace where a granite boulder was carved with a plain cross. The church is there to this day; it could be said that this was the first and certainly the humblest church that Arthur designed and constructed. Its very simplicity represents the importance of his religious belief in his life, and in those of his brothers. As recently as May 1990 a marriage service was held there by a minister of the United Reform Church following a registry office ceremony. Keble notes that the granite boulder was examined by the Devonshire Association some 40 years later and they decided that it was not mediaeval! (Colour Plate 2)

A few days after the camp ended Keble was getting married before taking up a new ministry at Wath upon Dearne, South Yorkshire. On July 8th he married Violet Chaworth-Musters at Ashbourne, Derbyshire; Arthur was his best man. His forthcoming marriage had not improved Keble's absent-mindedness; two days before the wedding he lost the wedding ring, which had been in his pocket. At the time they had all just returned from the Moor, so Jack set off towards the site of the camp to find it. It turned up shortly afterwards in Keble's pocket – wrapped in his handkerchief.

The following year, 1910, got off to a slow start. Charles Martin died at Dartington in February, and the family had to leave the Parsonage. Camp operations were directed from Longcause, between Dartington and Totnes, the home of Charles' sister Caroline and her nephew Willy, who was one of the regular campers. For the first time the campers had to apply to the Duchy of Cornwall for a licence to fish in the stream. Although the camp was on land belonging to Lord Churchill, the stream being the boundary, a licence had to be applied for and was duly granted.

Arthur again records kestrels, missel thrushes, grey wagtails as well as snipe and wheatears. Close to the camp a meadow pipit's nest was found with an almost full-grown young cuckoo in it, which 'resented discovery by violently pecking Arthur's finger'. A couple of days later the cuckoo, which had flown the nest, was discovered in the church still being fed by the pipits.

1910 was the last year that Arthur attended the camp, as he was to get married himself the following year, but the camps – and the diaries – continued annually until June 1913. By then the three brothers all had wives and families, and the Great War was about to change all their lives.

On a subsequent visit to the site of the camp some years later, Arthur was disappointed to find that Warren House had been abandoned. He was by then consulting architect to the Duchy of Cornwall – whose property extended well beyond that county – and was to become familiar with most of the older buildings on Dartmoor. A transcription of them is included as an appendix within this volume.

THE PRE-WAR YEARS

Arthur left Winchester in 1894 and was articled in London to the practice of E. J. May, who had himself been trained by R. Norman Shaw. Like all aspiring architects of his generation he travelled to Europe to explore the classic architecture of Italy and visit the great monuments of Antiquity. For two years from 1896 he studied at the Royal Academy School of Architecture, before setting up in independent practice in 1898.

This was the age of Edwardian elegance, when a yawning chasm separated the rich from the poor. Although not wealthy, Arthur's sartorial appearance, dry sense of humour and educated upbringing would have stood him in good stead in the drawing rooms of the upper classes at a time when many professional men relied largely on personal contacts to obtain new work.

One of his earliest commissions was the restoration of South Wraxall Manor in Wiltshire, a ten-bedroom, stone-built house described as 'one of the finest examples of Tudor, Elizabethan and Jacobean architecture in the south of England'. It is said that Sir Walter Raleigh and the owner at the time, Sir Walter Long, enjoyed here the first pipe of tobacco to be smoked in an English house.

The house had been unoccupied for 100 years, and this commission was a real coup for an architect so early in his career. The house is recorded in the listed buildings description as 'restored c.1900 by A. C. Martin for E. Richardson Cox Esq. JP.' Mr Cox was a government minister and had Rood Ashton as his seat; he was often in London and Ireland on affairs of state.

The house, which dates from the early fifteenth century, was held by the Long family until the early twentieth century. It seems that Cox agreed to have the work carried out on taking up the lease of the manor. An entry in Kelly's Directory of 1889 describes how the house 'at one period was leased to a Dr Knight, who kept a school there and much disfigured the house by plastering over the carved ceiling and painting the oak panelled wainscots: the present owner is endeavouring as far as possible to reinstate the mansion in its original style.' An article describing the completed restoration appeared in Country Life, March 26th 1904. In its full splendour, the manor has many exceptional features, including beautifully carved mantlepieces, fine wood panelling and decorative plasterwork. The Great Hall extends to the roof and has collar-beams on arched braces and raking queen posts. The Drawing Room has a tunnel-vault ceiling with delicate plasterwork tracery and a magnificent fireplace.

In the same year Arthur was commissioned to design an extension to Guisborough Hall in North Yorkshire, for Colonel Robert Chaloner, who was to become the first Lord Guisborough. The Museum records show that in the early eighteenth century the Chaloner family lived in the Old Hall in Bow Street; a contemporary engraving shows extensive formal gardens reaching almost to the Abbey ruins. It is said that the building was sold for scrap when Robert Chaloner was declared bankrupt in 1825. All that now remains of the previous estate is a ruined dovecote.

However the family's fortunes seemed to have taken a turn for the better. In 1904 they were reported to be living at Long Hull (or Hall) outside the town. The original house was built in 1857 by M. W. Teulon in the Jacobean Revival style with stone mullions and leaded-light casements. The roof has a balustraded parapet and grouped octagonal windows. Above the entrance is an attractive oriel window with a lead pyramidal roof and intricate vine decoration on the underside[1]. Arthur Martin extended the two-gabled frontage by half as much again, almost doubling the size of the building, and making an impressive country house on three floors, with as many as 28 bedrooms. Guisborough Hall is now a conference centre, although the interior retains all its original features and still has the feel of a family home. (Colour Plate 3)

Arthur's only book, *The Small House* was published in 1906 and is intended as a bridge between client and architect because 'one of his chief difficulties has been to impart to his client a proper understanding of the building he proposes to erect.' The definition of a small house is not one that would apply today, it is 'one designed for gentlefolk and their servants, but not costing more than £1000'. It discusses at length materials and layout, domestic arrangements and 'sanitary matters'. The kitchen arrangements are described in great detail:

> The pantry in a small house must be in close communication with the kitchen... since all the most delicate china and glass will be washed in the pantry, the sink should be made of wood and unlined; earthenware and lead-lined sinks are a frequent cause of breakage among such brittle articles. The parlour maid will also require nicely fitted cupboards for glass and china.

The appendix at the end places the book firmly in its own period:

> DRIVES should be 8 ft wide for a single vehicle. Two carriages can pass in a drive 11 ft wide. A two-horse carriage turns in 21 ft., but 30 ft should be allowed if possible.
> PATHS. To allow two to walk comfortably side by side the path should be 5 ft wide.
> LAWNS. For sowing a lawn, from two and a half to three bushels of grass seed are required per acre. A tennis lawn measures 78 ft long by 36 ft wide for a double court, or 27 ft for a single. Twenty feet should be allowed for running back at either end, and 10 ft at the sides. The service lines are 21 ft from the net. Badminton courts are 44 ft long and 20 ft wide; 10 ft should be allowed all round.
> BILLIARD ROOM: A billiard table measures 6 ft wide by 12 ft long between the cushions. An ordinary cue is about 5 ft long. The room should not be much less therefore than 24 ft long by 18 ft wide to enable every stroke to be played without hindrance.

Most of the houses in his book would by modern standards be regarded as substantial four and five-bedroomed homes. A house described as a seaside cottage has, in addition to hall, living room, dining room and kitchen, a scullery, pantry, veranda and loggia with five bedrooms above.

---

[1]National Monuments Record

THE PRE-WAR YEARS

Sketch for seaside cottage from The Small House.

On April 20th 1911 Arthur married Hope Johnston, the redheaded daughter of Alexander Johnston who was a merchant of the East India Line and is described as 'of Singapore'. They had met when Hope, a masseuse, had been treating a wrist injury suffered by one of the Awdry cousins; the occupation in those days did not have the overtones it carries today. They were married from the Awdry home at Market Lavington, Wiltshire. Arthur was already an avid birdwatcher: a fragile piece of paper that has survived in the family records lists the birds seen on their honeymoon. There are 62, which include:

Blackcap, Bullfinch, Chiffchaff, Corn Bunting, Dipper, Greenshank, Hawk, Jay, Linnet, Misselthrush, Nuthatch, Owl, Oystercatcher, Plover, Reed Bunting, Stonechat, Tree Creeper, Wheatear, Whitethroat, Yellowhammer.

The marriage was to last over 50 years; they had two children, Audrey born in 1913 and Michael, born in 1920.

In 1912 Arthur was elected a Fellow of the Royal Institute of British Architects 'from the class of Licentiates after passing the qualifying exam', and opened an office at 9 New Square, Lincoln's Inn. Much of his early work was with large country houses, and he claimed that he was one of the last architects to understand the requirements and workings of the large country establishment. One of his houses had 34 bedrooms providing accommodation for up to a dozen 'guns' with their ladies, ladies' maids, valets, etc. He was also commissioned to build a chapel for the Theological Hostel of King's College, London, which was in Vincent Square, the drawings for which were exhibited at the Royal Academy in 1913. Now known as Wellington Hall, the building is currently a general hostel for students at Kings'.

With the outbreak of war in August 1914 Arthur knew exactly where his duty lay. He enlisted as a private with the Royal Fusiliers on September 15th 1914 and was promoted to sergeant on November 30th. On New Years Day, 1915 he was commissioned as a second lieutenant and sailed for France with his unit in November that year to join the Western Front on La Bassée Canal.

We know little about his reactions to war service. For a man of gentle manner, brought up in the peaceful surroundings of a Devonshire parsonage the conditions must have been indescribable. He took with him a small handmade photograph album containing sepia photographs of his wife and daughter, as well as a tiny lock of golden hair tied with silk ribbon and labelled: OUR BABY GIRL 2.9.14.

A tiny surviving portion of a letter written to his wife is characteristically non-committal:

> I am still (8.0 pm 31 XII 15) in trenches, and now I am in the front line which is safer in so far as there are fewer shells in our immediate neighbourhood, the German line being so close, at one point only 60-70 yds... I have been asleep for 20 mins in my chair; my eyes are so heavy that it is positive pain to keep awake.
> Now I am writing from the school of instruction where I am to be till the 14th. It is 2 miles N.W. of the big town from...

Arthur's time at the front seems to have been short; on 29 May 1916, on his unit being broken up in France, he was appointed to the Staff College, Sandhurst, where he was to begin work on what he always regarded as his most important architectural commission.

Arthur was evidently brought back from the trenches specifically to undertake the refurbishment of the Royal Military College Chapel, but there seems to have been some confusion about whether he was employed as a consulting architect, or whether he was to continue on the payroll of the Army. In a letter dated November 1917 in which he is described as being a member of the College Instructional Staff, a member of staff with an illegible signature writes:

> Would it be possible to release him from Army Service, or place him on half pay, or in any other way make him available? He would not of course be paid out of Army funds during the time he is employed on the enlargement of the Chapel.

The reply came back:

> How long do you think he will be employed on this work? If it is likely to last till the end of the war we would gazette him out and give him an honorary rank. If it is for a shorter period or if the absolute relinquishment of his commission is undesirable we can merely strike him off Army pay.

He was not finally demobilized until May 1919 with the rank of Captain. He then returned to his architectural practice, which had relocated to 9 New Square, Lincolns Inn.

Keble, meanwhile, had gone to Christ Church, Oxford in 1896, where his father Charles had been a lecturer on Greek Philosophy. There was an expectation that Keble would study the same subject, and in order to do so he spent a year at Dartington after leaving school to study under his father's tuition. They came to an agreement that if Keble were to study Aristotle and Plato he could take a pass degree only, and take botany as another subject. 'This was to lubricate the Greek,' he was to say later. 'To make it a little bit easier.' He tells a story about Professor Dodgson, who as Lewis Carroll had written *Alice in Wonderland*; Alice was the daughter of a previous Dean. The professor was retired, but was still in and out of the college. Apparently Queen Victoria was so taken with *Alice* that she asked him to send her a copy of his next book, which he did. As he was a professor of mathematics it was a book on Differential Calculus.

Keble enjoyed his time at Christ Church, but he was very concerned about the expenses he was incurring:

> I was a great expense to my father, and I tried to keep down the College bills or battels. So for nearly three years my breakfast consisted of a bowl of porridge from the College kitchen at a penny, an egg from the creamery at Carfax, also a penny with bread and butter etc.

He was a keen member of the Volunteer Corps, and remembers two occasions when Royalty came to dine in Hall. The first was Edward Prince of Wales and Princess Alexandra; the second was Prince George, then Duke of York and Princess Mary, who the following morning inspected a parade of the Volunteer Corps.

He was able to pursue his interest in botany with Professor Vines at the Botanic Garden in Oxford, and it was here that he first made drawings, 'poor things that they were'. He was particularly interested in mosses, but he started drawing flowers 'because fellow students complained of the difficulty of identifying them from the long wordy descriptions in works then available'.

In his finals his viva voce exam was taken by Dr Spooner, whose conversation was greatly enlivened by listening for 'Spoonerisms'.

Soon after Keble took his degree the Boer War began, and a whole company of university men from the Volunteer battalion was going to South Africa. Keble would have liked to join them, but since he was by then intending to be ordained, he was persuaded that the two were incompatible. However his training in the Volunteer Corps stood him in good stead later when he was appointed chaplain of the Royal North Lancashire Regiment and later still when he served as a chaplain in the First World War.

Towards the end of 1899 the first drawing for the *Concise British Flora in Colour* was made at Dartington. It was of snowdrops against a background of ivy leaves, 'the first and last made against leaves not related to the flower,' and was soon followed by drawings of stitchwort and the geranium herb robert. Later he was to say that he liked to illustrate white or pale flowers against green foliage, as in a hedgerow.

While waiting for a place at Cuddesdon Theological College Keble spent two years as a private tutor. With one family he stayed in a local lodging and only went to the house for school hours, which must have been lonely; on his first evening he was invited to dinner, only to find that he, a member of the British Ornithologists' Union, was faced with a lark pie made with the legs of the birds sticking out through the pastry. It had been made as a special treat, and it is not difficult to imagine how Keble must have felt as he ate it.

His final job was outside Bovey Tracey on the slopes of Dartmoor. Here he was in his element:

> The top fence just above the house divided the woodland birds from those of the moor, the warblers from the chats, the tree pipits from meadow pipits. Greater spotted woodpeckers brought up a family in a poplar within a few feet of my bedroom window. We played tennis until the nightjars came out catching moths. I happened to find the strong new locality for the rare plant *Lobelia aurens*. Kew Herbarium and the Natural History Museum were supplied with specimens. I drew it and recorded it in the *Journal of Botany*, 1901, p 428. I well remember on fine Sunday mornings bicycling down to Bovey Tracey Church and pushing the bike up again 1,100 feet before breakfast.

In September 1901 Keble began what he calls his main life's work, when he joined Cuddesdon Theological College to prepare for the priesthood. It might also be described as his other life's work, in addition to the *Flora*. He was ordained deacon at the age of 25 on December 21st 1902, and having decided that after the woods and moors of Devon he should look for a post in an industrial parish, he was duly appointed as assistant curate in the parish of Beeston, an industrial suburb of Nottingham. It was a busy parish with a large Sunday School. Keble was expected to wear a top hat and frock coat even in high summer, and he recalls one year when the thermometer outside the vestry read 95 degrees. He was ordained priest on December 21st 1903 and continued to work at Beeston as assistant curate for a total of four years. It seems to have been a lonely life; the vicar had been taken ill and a large part of the visiting work fell on Keble. He lived in lodgings with his minimal possessions and missed the home companionship and intellectual conversation of a large family that he had been used to. He must also have sorely missed the fields and flowers of his beloved Devon, and the wild open spaces of the Moor.

In September 1906 he moved to Ashbourne, Derbyshire. On one Sunday morning he cycled to church at 7am to ring the 'rousing bell,' designed to wake the parishioners for the eight o'clock service. He entered the church to find smoke and sparks coming up through the floor beside the organ from the boiler-room underneath. He called the verger and together they managed to damp down the fire and shovel the smoking fuel out into the churchyard. Then, after a quick wash they returned to assist the vicar with the service in a smoky church. It was at Ashbourne that Keble lost his heart to a young lady in her twenties called Violet Chaworth-Musters, a talented piano-player whose family lived at Dove House in Ashbourne and were regular members of the church congregation. He managed to persuade his sister Dora to come on a visit, so that with suitable propriety he was able to invite Violet and her elder sister to tea. He must have concealed his feelings well, because soon after this when he proposed to Violet she was taken completely by surprise, and replied, 'I do not even know you, Mr Martin.' Some time later he was told that the family's response was, 'the Curate has proposed to Violet. What cheek!' However, the path of true love ran fairly smoothly, and in March 1908 Keble and Violet became engaged.

Violet's father, Henry Chaworth-Musters had a military moustache and was reputed to be somewhat erratic. He was fond of horses, and was often seen driving a high dogcart with whip and reins in hand. Those were the days of domestic servants, and one day he drove the 13 miles to Derby to bring a new cook back to Dove House. He put her on the back seat, but failed to remind her that in the back seat of a dog-cart you have to put your arm along the seat to hold on. When they arrived at Dove House the back seat was empty; history does not relate how far he had to go back towards Derby to retrieve his unfortunate passenger.

Keble and Violet were married on July 8th 1909, by which time Keble had been appointed to the benefice of All Saints, Wath upon Dearne near Rotherham, Yorkshire. The vicarage there had been built on old colliery workings and was uninhabitable, so for the first year, until a new vicarage was completed, they had to live in the next parish and Keble made the journey to Wath three or more times a day by bicycle or on foot. Keble writes:

> The Vicarage was condemned, and there was no building belonging to the Church where meetings of any kind could be held. The old vicarage had cracks an inch wide from the colliery workings, and we had to proceed to raise funds to build a new one. We used the old foundations, and kept the three cellars. Amongst the parochial records we found the original architect's plan of 1790. In this the cellars were labelled for three kinds of ale. Adjoining it was the brew house. There was no tea or coffee in those days, and the vicar was supposed to brew his own beer!

This was a busy time, with a lot of work to be done in the parish, and the flower drawing was temporarily on hold. In 1911 their first child Patrick arrived, followed two years later by Vivienne.

That same year the men of the Manvers Main Collieries had contributed generously to a new pulpit in the church, in memory of their former general manager, Joseph Frederick Thomsom, a churchwarden of the parish, who died on March 14th 1912. The pulpit, designed by Arthur Martin and carved by Arthur May, is richly decorated with a bird and vine design. The central figure of St Oswald has a sword in one hand and a cross in the other; Wath church had at one time been in the gift of St Oswald's Priory at Nostell. In 1911 the Archbishop of York, Cosmo Lang, dedicated the pulpit and the new Church House. The Archbishop evidently stayed the night with Keble and Violet, because he recounts this story:

> At ten o'clock at night the Archbishop was sitting in the drawing-room, and my wife's great friend Ida Askew said, 'Your Grace, would you like to go to your room now, because we want to put the ducks to bed.'

Ida Askew was a family friend who was a great help in the house and with the children.

On Thursday August 17th 1917 Keble and his parishioners were enjoying the annual Sunday School Treat in a field above Church House when a message reached him that the church was on fire. This was evidently more extensive than the fire at Ashbourne. Recounting the event in his book on Wath upon Dearne, Keble makes it sound much more serious:

> Starting in the vestry, which was gutted, the chancel roof was mostly destroyed, and the stonework in and above the vestry door arch. The organ was ruined and half the

The pulpit in All Saints, Wath upon Dearne, designed by Arthur Martin.

altar rail was burned. The nave roof was much charred and a hole burned near the middle aisle.

Keble was obviously puzzled as to why a fire should occur in high summer when there was no heating and no electrical appliances in use, and he was determined to find the culprit. It emerged that one particular boy had not been on the Sunday School Outing; a few days earlier the organist and choirmaster had called him a 'dirty little brute' and possibly smacked him. By setting fire to the surplices in the vestry and lighting a fire under the organ he had sought to wreak his revenge. The boy admitted his guilt and was sent to a reformatory for five years.

The repairs to the church had to wait until after the war, but in 1919 the nave roof was cleaned and repaired at a cost of £520 by Lazenby Bros of Leeds and the restoration of other parts was begun the same year. Later Keble notes that the architect for the work was Mr Arthur C. Martin of 9 New Square, Lincoln's Inn. In 1920 Keble published *A History of the Ancient Parish of Wath upon Dearne*, an indication of how deeply he was committed to his work in the area.

In his pastoral work Keble always attached great importance to visiting his parishioners, and even when he was an old man derived great pleasure from visiting people in their homes. Throughout his working life he kept careful abbreviated records which enabled him to use his visiting time effectively. It also helped him to include his parishioners in his prayers, something he felt led to real spiritual and practical guidance.

> We had learned to study quite a lot, in order to make sermons and class lessons really instructive. This study, and the consideration of its bearing on life, gave us useful thoughts in mind for the visiting. The first object of the visiting was to make friends with people, and to win their confidence by sympathy and mutual understanding. Then we could at least tell even those who were not members what the Church was thinking about that week. The visiting took long hours and was real work. We prayed for guidance in it. And we certainly sometimes had clear conviction of having received it.

The memory of Keble Martin is still held in great affection in Wath upon Dearne, where there is even a street named after him. His name on a beautifully inscribed List of Incumbents records that he was in the parish from 1909 – 1921. On the same board is a notice stating that the Dean and Chapter of Christchurch, Oxford, have been patrons of this benefice since 1540. Mrs Dorothy Hallatt, now aged 84, was christened by Keble, and another member of the congregation, Jim Thomson, recalls that his father sang in the choir in Keble's time.

Keble Martin Way, Wath upon Dearne.

The outbreak of the First World War found the Vicar of Wath with an increased workload, which included visiting the homes of the large numbers of men called up, and ensuring that the pastoral needs of the parish were met. There were food shortages, and one day they had to cycle to Doncaster, ten miles away, to get basic supplies for the children. By the end of the summer of 1916, 600 young men from Wath had gone to the war, and the number of losses was increasing. Many of these young men had never before left home, yet they were suddenly thrown into the maelstrom of a conflict from which millions would never return.

In the winter of 1917-18 there was a desperate call for more chaplains to join the army overseas. Keble was confident that the parish would be cared for in the hands of his curate and the clergy from two neighbouring parishes, so he approached the Bishop for permission to enlist, and this was granted. He presented himself for eight days of intensive training at Tidworth, only to find when he got there that he was the 10,000th recruit, and was given an inscribed First Aid book as a memento. He enlisted in the 34th Northumberland Fusiliers and joined them on the front line at Cassel, south of Dunkirk, where with a batman to carry a knapsack of service books he was able to hold services either in the open or in tents or barns 'with straw full of uninvited guests'. One of his duties was to write the difficult letters to the next of kin, often sitting for hours on a packing case in a draughty corner of a barn. To his parishioners he wrote:

> Do not make any mistake. The men long intensely for cleanliness and home, but there is a most noble spirit of self-sacrifice and endurance abroad. And they will stick to it. Pray for them. Under immense danger much brotherly kindness is being shown. Another side to it is that the birds are in full song and the flowers in full bloom. They are all our own familiar friends, the sweet English birds and flowers, robins, buttercups, daisies and others, reminding us how very near the fighting is to our own dear homes.

Keble himself was receiving bad news at this time, May 1918: his youngest son, Henry, whom he had last seen as a toddler pulling himself up to his mother's knee, was dangerously ill with meningitis. Keble was given compassionate leave, and walking into Wath on his way home from the station he met the road foreman, who expressed his sympathy at the little boy's death. Not telling him that he hadn't heard the dreadful news, Keble hurried home to comfort his wife.

After demobilization he returned to Wath, where in 1919 his daughter Lisette was born. The same year he completed the *History of Wath upon Dearne* which he had assembled during winter evenings from a sackful of old deeds, some dating as far back as 1300. By the summer of 1921 he had completed 12 years at Wath and the grimy atmosphere was affecting his daughter Vivienne's health. As it happened that summer there was a miners' strike, and almost for the first time the pall of dust that normally hung over the town cleared and they were able to see the Pennines.

That summer Keble was offered the benefice of Haccombe with Coffinswell, outside Newton Abbot. So it was that Keble brought his family back to Devonshire, and embarked on what was to be perhaps the most exciting and rewarding period of his life.

SANDHURST

When Arthur Martin was commissioned to redesign the Chapel at Sandhurst it was to be the third chapel at the College. The Royal Military College was moved from Great Marlow to Sandhurst in 1812, and the original chapel, a room opening out of the Grand Entrance, was in use for 67 years. It subsequently became a library and is now known as the Indian Army Memorial Room.

When the decision was made to build a separate chapel, the present site in front of the College Buildings was selected and the chapel was opened in 1879. It was known as Christ Church and was built as a memorial to those who devoted their lives to the service of their fellow men. The original chapel was designed by the Royal Engineers, who took their inspiration from a church in Florence. A scheme of decoration copied from the Cathedral Church of Siena was the inspiration for the interior, using a combination of alabaster and marble. In June 1883 a Memorial Fund was set up with the specific purpose of inscribing on special War panels the names of all those men who had passed through the College and had subsequently lost their lives in active service. By 1898 some 240 names were recorded, and by the time the Boer War had claimed another 262 lives of former cadets, it was rapidly becoming obvious that there was not enough room for further panels.

The New Buildings at the College were completed in 1911, and with the threat of war on the horizon and the number of cadets more than doubled from 350 to over 700, Christ Church was totally inadequate for the needs of the college. Services had to be doubled to accommodate the cadets, and there was not enough room for visiting families and friends.

With the outbreak of war the plans had to be shelved, but towards the end of the Great War it was proposed by the Commandant, Sir Lionel Stopford that the chapel should be rebuilt as a memorial chapel to those cadets who had lost their lives in the Great War. It had always been a tradition at the College that the names of all cadets who fell on active service were inscribed on the chapel walls, but with more than 4,000 cadets lost in the Great War, there was simply not enough room available.

Captain Martin approached this project with his usual reserve and modesty, but also with great enthusiasm. It offered a challenge and an opportunity for innovative design which he was more than equal to. His proposed concept for the chapel was truly inspirational. Rather than demolish the existing chapel, he drew up plans in which the enlarged chapel was to be built across the old, so that the previous building became the transepts of the new. This of course altered the orientation of the building, but since this was simply from south-east to north-east there was no problem. In this way the west end and the apse of the old chapel were preserved, along with the memorials to those who had lost their lives in earlier conflicts, including the Crimean and South African Wars. In the new chapel the seating accommodation was increased from 420 to

1,000 to accommodate the greater number of cadets while new panels would bear the names of those who fell in the Great War. In 'The Chapel' by Blackburne and Waring, published in 1922 it states:

> The fitness and the beauty of these plans were quickly appreciated, and an eminent architect was asked for his criticisms on them. He received them with great praise, and declared that the whole conception was a stroke of genius.

An article in *The Times* of 17 February 1919 comments:

> Altogether the proposed building promises to be a beautiful one, lofty, impressive and of graceful proportions, white marble pillars and panels being set off by dark oak, and the eye of the worshipper being carried to a large silver cross above the altar. Piers and columns of marble, domes of mosaic, and stained glass windows will contribute to the dignity of the completed chapel. Provision for the thousands of names to be recorded is made in the memorial panels, which are an essential part of the decoration. Regimental grouping will be adopted for these names and each list will be surmounted on the marble of the panels by the regimental crest and badge. The name of no Sandhurst who died in the war will be omitted.

With the approval of the Army Council Captain Martin's plans were accepted, and were later exhibited at the Royal Academy. The new committee then turned its attention to raising the necessary funds. The timing of the new project was unavoidable but unfortunate. In the initial discussions which were interrupted by the war, it had been expected that the cost would come out of public funds. However in the aftermath of the war the picture had changed drastically and there was to be no help from the Exchequer for a project that could hardly be described as essential in the post-war climate.

The cost was estimated at £50,000, of which £5,500 had already been contributed to a Memorial Fund. This excluded the cost of promised memorials to individuals and to regiments. Because of the financial problems it was decided to carry out the work in four stages: the laying of the foundations, the east end, the conversion of the existing chapel into the centre part of the new building, and finally the west end. The contract was awarded to Messrs Holloway Brothers of Westminster, and in the autumn of 1918 work on the new foundations started. They were completed the following spring, but because of a lack of funds the work then stopped for a year. The reason for starting the work on this ad hoc basis was that following a public appeal a number of gifts and private memorials had been promised, and it was felt that some donors would not be prepared to wait indefinitely for the work to get under way.

In December 1919 Major-General R. B. Stephens, who had succeeded General Stopford, launched a public appeal for £10,000 to enable the next stage to continue. On March 1st, 1920 work on the new east end began. It was completed the following year and opened by the Archbishop of Canterbury on May 5th 1921. In the same year a huge fund-raising fete was held which realised the tremendous sum of £6,000. It was organised by the Chaplain, H. W. Blackburne, who had been Chaplain in the early part of 1914 and returned to Sandhurst in 1917. It was his dedication, energy and enthusiasm that kept the fund-raising in the public eye as he watched his beloved chapel take shape.

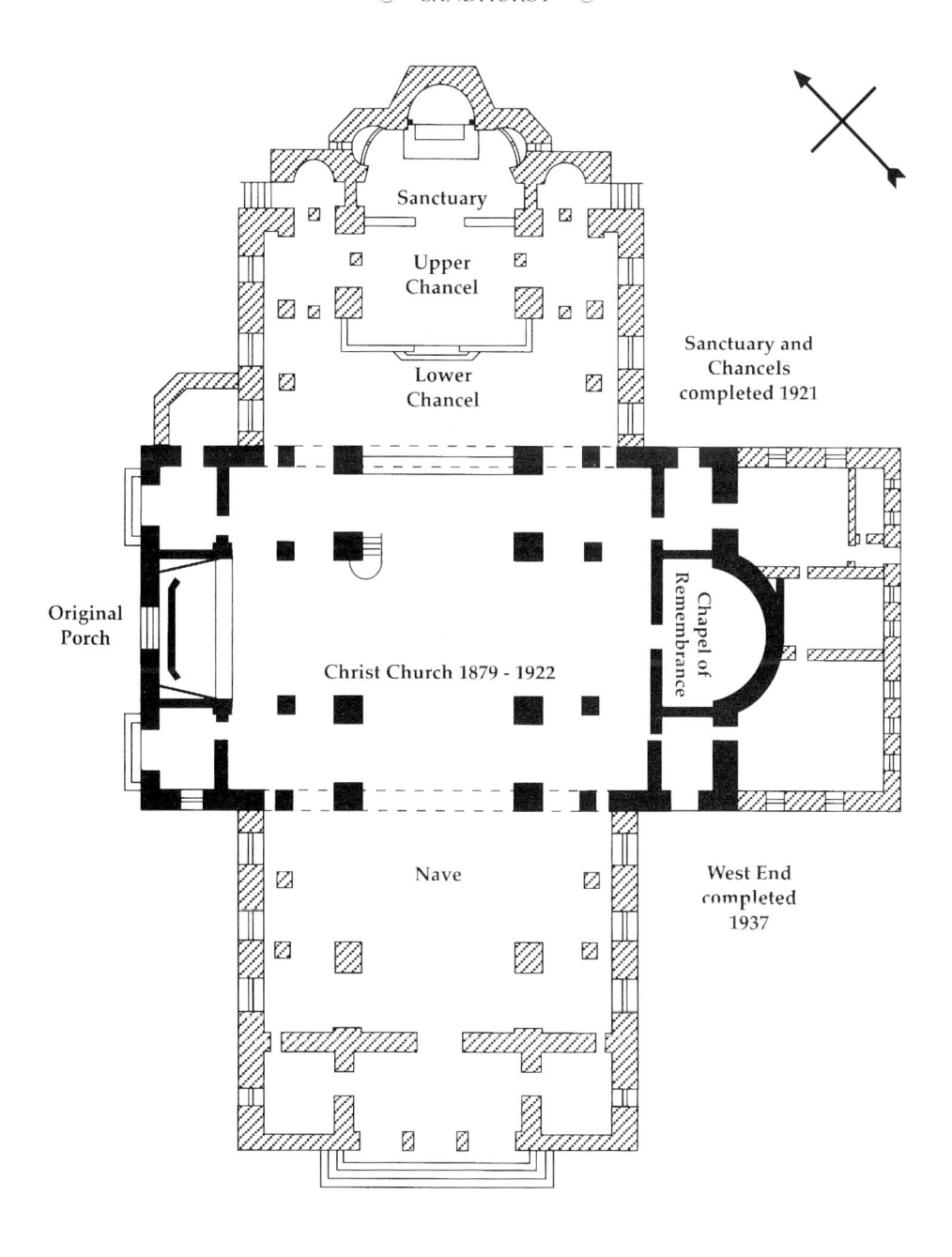

SANDHURST

Ground plan of the Royal Memorial Chapel, Sandhurst.
(Crown Copyright/MOD. Reproduced with the permission of Her Majesty's Stationery Office)

The dedication of the Royal Memorial Chapel showing King George VI talking to the Archbishop of Canterbury with the architect, Arthur Martin (centre).
(Sandhurst Collection and Royal Memorial Chapel)

After another interval of a year on May 9th 1922 work started on the central section as the original building was altered to fit the new design. The organ was renovated and moved to its new position over the porch of the old chapel. Meanwhile fund-raising continued, and by the time Harry Blackburne retired, £54,000 had been raised and expended on the rebuilding and a modest £2,000 was all that remained for the completion of the work.

By 1933 the balance in hand was £3,500, and a major effort was launched to get the building completed. A number of charity events and a successful appeal to the public raised this sum to £6,000. Finally through the intervention of Lord Halifax, Lord Privy Seal and former Secretary of State for War, a grant of £10,000 from public funds enabled the fourth and final stage to get under way in July 1936. The architect's original plans had included a tower rising centrally above the nave, but the depression of the 1930s made any further fund-raising unrealistic, and the tower was abandoned.

The new west doors to the chapel were given by the officers and cadets of the College 'in memory of King George V and his courageous reign'. Arthur Martin always said with wry humour that he and Queen Mary had very different ideas about the design of the memorial doors, and that Queen Mary won.

On 2nd May 1937 the completed chapel (Colour Plate 4) was dedicated by the Archbishop of Canterbury in the presence of King George VI and Queen Elizabeth, accompanied by Queen Mary and the Princess Royal. A photograph of that date clearly shows Arthur Martin in a group with the King and the event was reported in *The Times* Court Circular the following day.

It was to be another sixteen years before much of the detailed work on the chapel was completed. *The Times* of October 28th 1950 reported on the dedication of the memorial pews and the organ in the presence of the Duke of Gloucester:

> The dedication ceremony was conducted by the Chaplain-General to the Forces, Canon F Hughes, who spoke of the radiant honour with which the officers now commemorated had met danger, of their mastery of themselves and their leadership of men. As the service ended the Last Post and Reveille were sounded and pipers played a lament.

Among the documents which have survived in the Sandhurst archives is the Bill of Works, written in copperplate, for £25,987.0s.0d. There are detailed instructions to the plasterer and painter and the closing words:

> Ornamental hopper heads £8.0.0 pc including nails and collars. Doors in English oak well seasoned. 'Make good and leave perfect.'

The Royal Memorial Chapel as it stands today is an elegant and fitting tribute to the thousands of young men who gave their lives for their country in two world wars as well as other conflicts. The architecture of the chapel follows the Byzantine style of Northern Italy, as did the style of the original chapel. The vaulted roof is lit by high windows and supported on square pillars, giving a lofty, well-lit effect, and the combination of white marble with oak woodwork and pews is quite unique. (Colour Plate 5)

Above the cross which hangs over the altar is a striking semi-dome which was the work of Mr Anrup, a Russian, and was completed in 1921. The subject is taken from Revelations Chapter I, '...one like unto the Son of man... His head and his hairs were white like wool, as white as snow; and his eyes were as a flame of fire... and he had in his right hand seven stars; and out of his mouth went a sharp two-edged sword; and his countenance was as the sun shineth in his strength.' In the left hand are seven stars representing seven churches, and in the right hand are the keys of Death and Hades. It is one of the few examples of genuine Russian mosaic in the country and was executed without trace or copy, following the methods used in early Christian churches. It was presented as a private memorial.

The memorial panels which were pivotal to the concept of rebuilding the chapel form a striking feature of the design. Earlier memorials remain within the Chapel of Remembrance, which formed the sanctuary of the previous chapel; it has white alabaster panels on either side of the altar, depicting the Incarnation and the Resurrection, which were copied from St Paul's Cathedral, while the altar and the reredos form part of the memorial to the dead of the South African War. In front of the altar the Book of Remembrance records the names of those former cadets who have died while serving since 1947.

The names of those cadets who gave their lives in the Great War are carved into the white marble pillars and panels of the new nave and chancel. Each panel was presented by the regiment concerned, with every regiment in the British Army responding to the appeal; the panels are topped by the regimental crest in full colour carved from the marble, with the names coloured and each panel outlined in bronze. Below is a simple dedication which in most cases includes a tribute to those other ranks who gave their lives in the Great War. The panels for the line regiments are mostly in the body of the chapel; those for the foot guards on the right of the chancel and those for the cavalry on the left. There are also a number of individual memorials; to read them is a poignant reminder of how young were many of those who died.

After the Second World War further memorials were planned to commemorate the fallen officers of the Commonwealth. Oak pews were commissioned to complete the seating in the chancel and nave, each bearing the crests or badges of the corps and Regiments of the British and Commonwealth armies. These badges, finely carved and painted on the pew ends, were designed by Captain Martin himself.

In front of the chancel steps is the Roll of Honour, which records the names of nearly 20,000 officers who gave their lives during the Second World War. Each Sunday a page is turned at the beginning of Morning Service. An oak panel in the nave lists the conflicts fought since 1945; the cost in lives has been high: 1968 was the only year since World War II when no lives were lost.

Among the other notable memorials are the windows, which were the result of an appeal in 1959. They were designed by Lawrence Lee; in the nave there are two sets of memorial windows to Field Marshals and four windows presented by regiments: the Brigade of Guards, the Royal Northumberland Fusiliers, the Hampshire Regiment and the Rifle Brigade. Other regiments donated the black marble paving in the chancel, which are such a superb foil to the decoration of the chapel as a whole. The marble steps up to the chancel were donated as private memorials; one in fact is not a memorial at all but a thanksgiving for a life preserved, another is a tribute of sympathy from the cadets of West Point, USA.

The silver font in the Baptistery was the gift of the Machine Gun Corps. So it is that everything that meets the eye on entering the chapel is the gift of a regiment or corps, or a donation in tribute to a loved individual. Even the bricks and mortar were the product of private subscription and generosity.

Outside the west door stands a memorial in bronze to the rank and file of the British Army who fell in both World Wars, a tribute to the courage and devotion of those Other Ranks and a reminder of the bonds of loyalty between officers and men.

Sandhurst Chapel is also a memorial to the vision and inspiration of the architect, Arthur Campbell Martin. From Blackburne and Waring's book comes a closing tribute:

> Not only is the main structure the work of the architect, but almost every detail of the interior as well. Possibly praise of the architect may seem an obvious commonplace in a book like this, especially as it comes from those who with no great knowledge of his art, but with an intense interest in his endeavours, have watched his work growing day by day. Still, he has earned the highest praise from those who have the knowledge, and it must appeal to all that the master mind belongs to one who worked for the College and took part in its daily life in the strenuous times of war.

HACCOMBE AND COFFINSWELL

For the period of more than 30 years while the chapel at the Royal Military College was under construction, Arthur had plenty of other work on his hands. With the changes in social patterns after the Great War much of his larger domestic work came to an end. He built a large number of medium-sized houses, including two for his own family in Englefield Green and six others in the same area. His daughter, then aged about seven, remembers being taken up into the roof at Courtways, the first house that he built for himself, and being lectured on the intricacies of the various joints in the rafters. Among her earliest memories is the status of becoming a car-owning family when they bought their first car, a Model-T Ford.

Arthur and his wife Hope first came to Englefield Green in about 1920, when they leased Shelley's Cottage from Alice Liddell of Alice-in-Wonderland fame. Commoners, the second house he built for his family in 1927-8, was the name given to the non-Scholars at Marlborough College. Not far from Courtways, it was a substantial house befitting his professional position. However they had no resident staff, with a woman from the village coming in daily as a cleaner. As was the norm in those days he and Hope did a good deal of entertaining, bringing in local domestic staff for the occasion. Their daughter Audrey, whose bedroom was the centre window in the front, was married from this house.

Like most professional men of some standing, he was an active and hard-working member of the community. At one time or another he held every office in the parish that was open to a layman, including representing the Diocese at the Church Assembly (now the Synod). It was his initiative that led to the parish of St Jude's, Englefield Green, being created a separate parish in 1930. He not only had a strong Christian faith; his innate humility and deference to others made him a highly respected figure in the parish. He was also non-confrontational: he would back down from an argument even when he knew he was in the right.

He built a total of eight vicarages, of which one was in Englefield Green and another at Milber, outside Newton Abbot, for the parish of the 'Dream Church'. Many of his houses are recognisable by his use of plain arches and cross-vaulted ceilings in halls and passageways. In all his work there is a feeling of intimacy produced by rounded arches creating an interesting play of light and shade. Among the smaller houses he designed was a terrace in Budleigh Salterton, Devon, known as The Lawn. Pevsner describes it as 'an engaging mock-mediaeval terrace stepping down the hill. A lively design of repeated asymmetrical units in a picturesque mixture of materials: roughcast, stone-mullioned bay window, half-timbering and a large two-light cusped wooden window, red tiled gables to add a touch of colour: 1935 by A. C. Martin'.[1] Sherwood House, in the same town, is described as 'an overblown twentieth-century version of a cottage orné, well detailed, but without Gimson's finesse'.

---

[1] Pevsner. *The Buildings of England.*

Left: *Interior of Courtways, the first house that Arthur built for himself and his family at Englefield Green. Note the characteristic plain arches.*

Below: *Commoners, the second house Arthur designed for his family.*

Arthur always regarded his major work in London as the rebuilding of the east wing of the Duchy of Cornwall offices in Buckingham Gate after the building was bombed in the Second World War. Amazingly, no-one was killed or injured when the bomb fell, in spite of the extensive damage. The building was originally designed by Sir James Pennethorne in 1854, and Arthur's plans followed his Italianate style with a richly detailed classical facade, as befitted a building that faces Buckingham Palace. Being on a corner, the building has a splayed corner block with Doric columns to the portico. The first floor has a balustraded balcony; the windows have Corinthinian columns and pilasters, and pediments with dentil moulding over the central windows. Above the second-floor windows is a handsome decorative frieze.

Inside, the formal rooms have classical fireplaces and elegant fittings, with the Council Room large enough to accommodate an enormous oval table. Upstairs, what would have been the servants' quarters is now a sizeable flat. Here Arthur's eye for domestic detail comes into its own: the plans required a servants' lift, and an Aga as well as a gas cooker.

He had been appointed as consultant architect to the Duchy in 1927. It was a job he enjoyed enormously; it took him back to his beloved Devonshire (Duchy properties amounting to 26,000 acres did then and still do extend well beyond the boundaries of Cornwall). Jock Stanier, who was Land Steward for the Duchy, as was his father, remembers Arthur with affection: his dry sense of humour, his extensive knowledge and love of wildlife and his courtesy to everyone he met, however humble. His role was purely advisory; the Duchy was not subject to planning laws, and he would have been consulted regularly on all matters relating to the repair and maintenance of buildings and new developments as and when required. One of these was a sizeable estate for Duchy workers and their families at Stoke Climsland, Cornwall.

Arthur Martin served as architect to the Duchy for 25 years until his retirement in 1952, and was awarded the CVO for his services.

Throughout his life Arthur was a strong churchman and derived great pleasure and spiritual satisfaction from church work. In the parish of St Mary's, Speen, near Reading, his architect friend Walter Medlicott from Dartmoor days lived in the village and his wife was on the Parish Council. Arthur was commissioned by Mrs Edwards to design a reredos for the church in memory of her late husband, Vicar of Speen. The Parish Council minutes of August 16th 1924 record how Arthur Martin had emphasized that the woodwork would require a very experienced craftsman, and that he could recommend a Mr May of London[2]. The reredos was dedicated on July 11th 1926. Some years later in 1945 in memory of a subsequent vicar, Arthur designed a screen for the choir vestry and produced plans for proposed repairs to the sanctuary. In the event, however, the only work carried out was repaving of the floor to the sanctuary; the rest was abandoned because of the high cost.

Keble and his family moved from the industrial area outside Sheffield to the rural rectory at Coffinswell, outside Newton Abbot, in the last week of July 1921. The change must have been startling, especially to their small children. Keble reports:

---

[2] This was possibly the same Mr May who had carved the pulpit at Wath upon Dearne.

The bomb-damaged frontage of the Duchy offices in Buckingham Gate.
(Duchy of Cornwall Library & Archives)

The Duchy offices today.

Arthur Martin's plan for the rebuilt Duchy offices.

> The grass on the fields and lawns was brown and dry. Just as the furniture arrived at the rectory, the sky opened up. We had a drenching thunderstorm, water everywhere. The little rectory drive was made of gravel bedded in stiff yellow clay, and this was trodden freely to every corner of the newly scrubbed house. All had to be scrubbed again. The place was attractive. There was a large garden which had to be maintained, and a tennis court made by my brother, who had been there before us.

Keble was duly instituted as Archpriest of Haccombe and Rector of Coffinswell, an office he was to hold for over 12 years.

> I was always alone for the 8am daily office at Coffinswell, where I read the psalms and lessons aloud, which I found helpful. Yet I was not always quite alone: small winged visitors frequently came and joined in. There was a rat hole under the tower door and the local robins and wrens knew all about it, and came to clear insects or spiders from the windows, and then sometimes sat on the pulpit near me to sing loudly, as if to drown my voice. A pair of wrens also came into Haccombe Church and built a nest in the carving under the pulpit.

This picture of the gentle parson, a passionate nature-lover, reading the Psalms to the birds in an empty church is one which captures the imagination. He had a strong, wiry physique, and apparently used to run between the two parishes in an attempt to keep himself fit.

After the heavily populated parish he had come from, Keble found the work in his new parish much less demanding. He was able to spend more time with his family and even to take holidays, as gradually his collection of drawings was built up. On one occasion when they were staying with friends on the Norfolk Broads he hired a small rowing boat to collect a specimen of *Carex pseudo-cyperus*. As he approached a small island the resident swans took exception to this intrusion and attacked him noisily. However he managed to stay afloat and returned triumphant with his specimen.

His daughter Lisette remembers that they used to have family picnics in the Devon countryside, but as soon as they arrived Keble would disappear to do what the children called his 'botanising' and not return until the party was packing up to go home. On these occasions he always carried a set of three little boxes with glass bottoms, and usually returned to the picnic with something in his boxes to show the children.

'I hate spiders and creepy things,' Lisette recalls, 'but always enjoyed looking at them in the boxes because I knew he wouldn't let them out and frighten me.'

He always carried a walking stick, even in Dartington days, which he used for a number of purposes apart from the obvious one, such as pulling down blackberry stems so that the children could reach the fruit. He used it on several occasions to separate the family terrier in a fight with another dog, and on one occasion he hurled it at a fox, catching it on the neck so that it dropped the chicken it was carrying.

Lisette recalls that he was often helping out in local disasters. When there was a train crash close to Milber he rushed off on his bike to see what he could do. And on another occasion when a thatched house caught fire he again dashed off to help get the family's possessions out of the burning house. Periodically there were fires on Milber Common, and he was always there if there was any trouble, or any danger to the public.

His drawings advanced rapidly and the first 12 plates for what was to become the *Concise British Flora in Colour* were completed during this period. The drawings were first made in the form of pen outlines on small separate sheets and then assembled in groups, with as many as fifteen on one plate. The pen-and-ink drawings, on thin paper, were kept in a loose-leaf file, and getting several drawings fitted on to one plate was a difficult operation. He would pin a sheet of white paper to the wooden crossbar of a window, and juggle a number of drawings about behind it in order to fit as many as possible on to one plate and trace them off. As this was best done with the sun behind it, another sheet of white paper was positioned above the window bar to keep the sun out of his eyes.[3] There were often gaps on the plates where he had not been able to get hold of a particular specimen; sometimes the gap would not be filled for twenty years or more, and often meant that the entire plate had to be redesigned to accommodate it.

Towards the end of his time at Milber, a note in Keble's autobiography gives some idea of the mammoth size of the undertaking. In the winter evenings of 1932-3 he and his wife gave serious consideration to the possibility of completing the one hundred hand-painted plates of flowers, and an estimate was made of the work done and the work yet to be done. The results were not encouraging: a painstaking survey of the work showed that out of about 1480 figures proposed only 677, or less than half had been drawn. Also the amount of new work had fallen: in 1927 some 66 figures had been added, while in 1932 only 24 were drawn.

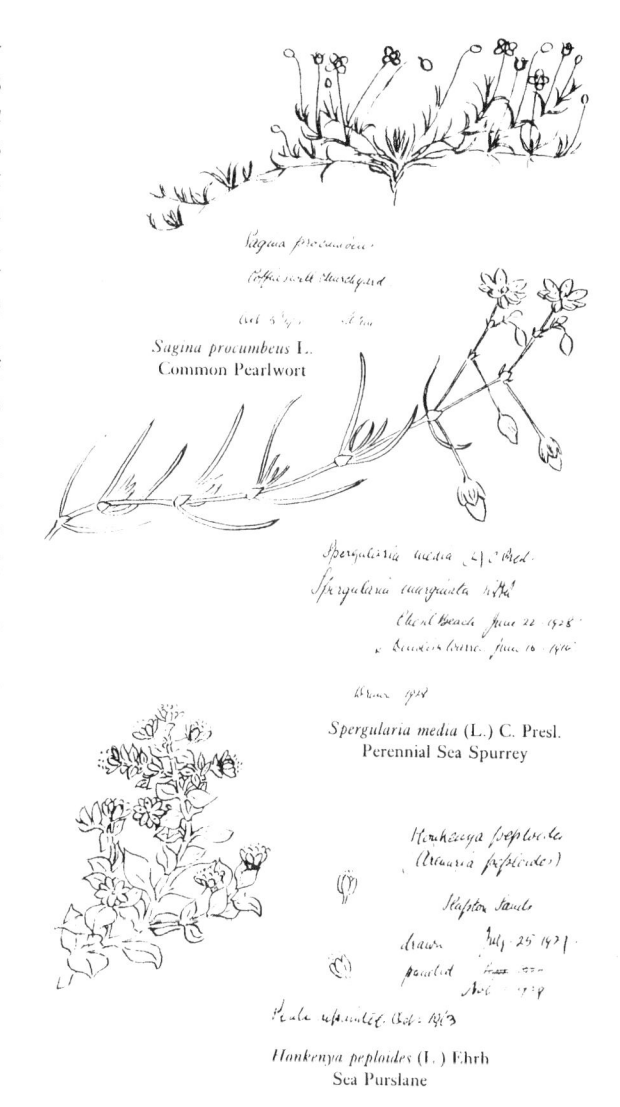

Some of Keble's original sketches for the Flora
(by permission of the Linnean Society of London)

---

[3]The drawings from the loose-leaf files were reproduced after his death in a book called *Sketches for the Flora* published by Michael Joseph in 1972. The originals of the drawings are held by the Linnean Society.

This was largely due to the increased parochial work created by the new housing estates in the parish, and also partly due to the repainting of earlier plates. The paper used for the earlier work had been of poor quality, and since 1924 all the work had been redrawn and repainted on better paper. He was also having problems obtaining some of the rarer specimens, and lists of those required were issued to the Botanical Exchange Club, to which several members responded. Often a first drawing was made from a posted specimen and later redrawn when he was able to find a specimen of his own.

> Thus the figures on the plates, as we see them, were not always completed in a single effort. To look at the first plate only, and the little figure at the top: *Thalictrum alpinum* was first drawn from a specimen gathered on Ben Lawers in Perthshire by Mr Helsby in 1927. In the following year I saw it on Widdlebank Fell, a leaf was added and the figure much improved. Then the whole plate was traced, retraced and re-painted in 1932. How to do the work had to be learned the harder way, without help.

Later he recalls another hurried visit to Perthshire, which shows how reluctant he was to remove rare plants from their habitat:

> After a full Sunday, 24 July 1933, the midnight train took me to Killin and Ben Lawers. There the clouds were down to 1,000 feet. I went straight up in the clouds and rain and chanced to find two nice saxifrages, one especially which is very local and flowers sparingly. *Saxifragia cernua* is so rare it doesn't have an Engish name. It was in flower, so I took it down and made a drawing and coloured it. The next morning, up in mist and rain again I luckily found its own niche and replanted it firmly in its own place. A few other little alpine species were gathered and these were all in cigarette tins. They were all drawn in the train during Thursday night on the return journey. The trick is to have your elbows tight against your side and to sway with the train.

Keble had been elected a Fellow of the Linnean Society in 1928 and was an enthusiastic member of the Devonshire Association, which had a newly-founded Botanical Section. Keble's name appears frequently in their Transactions, usually in connection with an obscure plant that he had located. Together with Gordon T. Fraser he edited the *Flora of Devon*, published in 1939, an exacting and erudite study of the subject which was to make him a household name. He was also working on a history of the parish of Coffinswell, which was published by the Devonshire Association some years later. It is a detailed and technical account of the history of the parish, including field names, manor records, census returns and parish records.

Above: *Plate 1.
All Saint's Church,
Wood Norton,
painted by Dora Martin.*

Left: *Plate 2.
The Dartmoor
chapel as it is today.*

Plate 3. Guisborough Hall, North Yorkshire.

Plate 4. The Royal Memorial Chapel, Sandhurst.
(Crown Copyright/MOD. Reproduced with the permission of the Controller of Her Majesty's Stationery Office)

Plate 5. Interior of the Royal Memorial Chapel.
(Sandhurst Collection and Royal Memorial Chapel)

Plate 6. Father John Potter of St Luke's, Milber, wearing a cope embroidered with designs from the Flora.

Plate 7. St Luke's, Camberwell. Altar designed by Arthur Martin. (A. Stocker)

Plate 8. The Concise British Flora in Colour.

Plate 9. Keble Martin on the day he received his honorary degree at Exeter University. (Source unknown)

Plate 10. Stamps from the Flora *issued by the Post Office.*

THE DREAM CHURCH

It was during Keble's earlier days at Coffinswell that new housing developments which were being built for Newton Abbot Urban District Council were springing up in the neighbouring parish of Milber, on the hill above what is now the busy A380. Milber had no place of worship; it was part of the ecclesiastical parish of Combe-in-Teignhead where the Rector, Mr Pound was elderly and had only a pony as a means of transport for parish visiting. Since the village of Milber was three miles and two hills away, Keble, with the Bishop's permission, undertook the visiting on the new housing estate. This was time-consuming, but Keble was interested in meeting new people and always found parish visiting one of the most enjoyable aspects of his work. And so began for Keble what was to be a long and fruitful association with the infant parish of Milber. Here, over 30 years later he was to see the realisation of a dream that he and his brother Arthur were to build together.

In 1928 the development company that was building the new estates offered as a gift a small site for a church. However Keble felt it was too small, also it had a gravel pit in the middle so he persuaded the Bishop that it was not suitable. He then wrote to the Earl of Devon at Powderham Castle, who was the major landowner in the Milber area. His request was successful, and the Earl offered a two-acre site for £300. After consultation with the planning authority the offer was accepted and the site on which the church and vicarage now stand was agreed upon. The Deed of Conveyance is still among the parish records, dated the First Day of October One thousand nine hundred and twenty six.

> From the Right Honourable the Earl of Devon: A Vest in Deed, hereinafter called the Principle Vest in Deed of the Conveyance to the Diocesan Board of Finance of a five-acre piece of Land[1] part of the Milber Estate, Newton Abbot in the County of Devon. Managers have agreed with the vendor to purchase from him a fee simple estate in possession free from encumbrances hereafter described for the price of Three Hundred Pounds.

Earlier houses near the church at the time had it written into their deeds that 'they shall not hold meetings of the Mormons or Jehovah's Witnesses, or complain about the bells'. There was also a clause agreed with the vendor that for 21 years the property shall never be used for purposes other than the scheduled purposes, and shall never be used as a burial ground. This was to protect the land in front of the church from being sold for housing.

---

[1] This possibly refers to the whole site including the churchyard, a corner of which was later sold for housing.

The need for a building on the newly-acquired site as a focal point for social and Christian fellowship was paramount, and the parish embarked on major fund-raising events in much the same way as was happening at Sandhurst, but on a less public scale. Milber was then still a small parish, but under Keble's guidance a strong Christian fellowship developed in the community, and much of the manual work was undertaken by the men of the parish. In February 1930 a wooden mission room, affectionately known as The Hut, was opened on the church site, and licensed by the Bishop. It was a dual purpose building, designed as much for social events as for worship, because as Keble said, social gatherings have their proper and essential place in church life. It had a small sanctuary which could be shut off, and in front of the sanctuary a raised platform. At the opening ceremony on February 26th 1930 it was arranged for visiting dignitaries to sit on this platform, among them Lord Devon, who was almost eclipsed by the large surpliced figure of Archdeacon Cobham.

The Bishop of Exeter in his address said, 'These are the days of small things. There is a lot of work to do here.' He also blessed the Holy Table given by the mother church of Combe, and the communion vessels which were a gift from Keble's brother Jack, then Rector of Dartington.

The new parish was heavily in debt: for the site as well as £400 for the cost of the mission room. The existing clergy had to cover the services in the new church in addition to those at Haccombe and Coffinswell. This meant that there were often seven services on a Sunday, starting with 7.30am Communion at Coffinswell, and ending with 7pm Evensong at Milber. The work at Milber was unpaid, apart from the Easter Offerings which were given by Keble to the Curate-in-Charge to help towards travelling expenses. Keble writes:

> For about eight years the work was voluntary...we had no idea of suggesting that the work should be paid for. Not that it was a case of a rich man being well able to give his services. In this and the three following years, it was not easy. In spite of frugal living the bank account was more often than not overdrawn, with all that this involved in the way of pledges to the bank. We saw the need for work at Milber and the opportunity of doing it. And this was surely a call to fulfil it. It would have been wrong not to have done it. So it was no work of supererogation, as somebody called it. Voluntary work becomes a deep source of happiness for us all.

The following year, on the morning of 11th March, 1931, Keble woke with the distinct recollection of a dream. There had been some trouble in the parish with a group of young hooligans from Newton Abbot, and some personal animosity towards the clergy, although not from the members of Milber Church. In the dream Keble was preaching in a new church building from the chancel step; the church was full of people and was of a curious pattern. The altar behind him was in a round stone apse; in front of him were three diverging naves, one unfinished. From the centre nave a man approached him as if to attack him; he was apprehended by the warden and sidesmen, who took him out through the north nave, which was full of people, and 'cast him into the outer darkness'.

So vivid was the dream to Keble that on waking he drew a sketch of the church and decided to send it to his brother Arthur, the architect, to see if the unorthodox plan was at all feasible. With it he sent the following hastily scribbled note:

THE DREAM CHURCH

Coffinswell Rectory
Newton Abbot
11 March 1931

My dear Arthur,

I had an odd and vivid dream last night, part of which was architectural, so I pass it on to you. I related it when I woke. I was in a new and unfinished church, preaching from the altar step, for there was no pulpit and no suitable place for one. It was such an odd church, but a man with a very hateful face came up the steps threatening me. The church was full of people. When he reached the top step I was, dreamlike, on the Altar, standing where the Office should be, airy-like, not irreverent, nor with any mundane shoe. As he came nearer I stepped back on to a Glastonbury chair, the seat of which was almost level with the altar. The altar was large, with very massive projecting and carved ends, eight or nine inches thick black oak, with its ornaments in place.

I waved with a little book of sermon notes (a thing I do not use) to the Secretary of the Church Council (Langford) who was sitting in the pew marked 1, and to the tallest man in the Council (Phillips) in pew 2. They at once responded and came to apprehend the man with threatening aspect. Other men stepped out, all sidesmen, twelve in all, and handed the brawler over to the two smallest men of their company, who held his wrists and marched him down the north transept followed by the other ten in procession. As they moved off with him I only said to him, 'We must behave ourselves here as we must in heaven.'

The odd thing was that the north transept was in direct line with me just as the nave aisle was. The pews were full. The south transept was bricked off unfinished, and the apse (no east window) white dressed stones intended to be decorated. The people vanished, and as I went out the porch appeared to be between the transepts beyond a connecting alley. That is all. I imagine the windows were round-topped and high up, but the brawling was at an evensong.

I have completed the church a little in the free-hand plan. Impossible structurally I do not doubt.

I hope you are well and thriving. I was off duty on Sunday but am quite well again. Frosty here too.

With much love
y.l.b.
W. KEBLE MARTIN

PS. Of course I have had a lot of happy dealings with these men over the last three years. I do preach from the altar step, in front of a little old Jacobean altar, and I have just been negotiating the purchase of a Jacobean chair. The organ and choir are on my right or north side, but the brawler and the radiating transepts are only of the dream. I was reading some history a few weeks ago in Bingham's 'Antiquities' and saw some plans of churches with apse and chairs all round.

The church of Keble's dream was unconventional, to say the least. There was no chancel and no screen to divide the sanctuary from the nave. The sanctuary opened into a broad central area from which three naves led off, like the point of an arrow. This

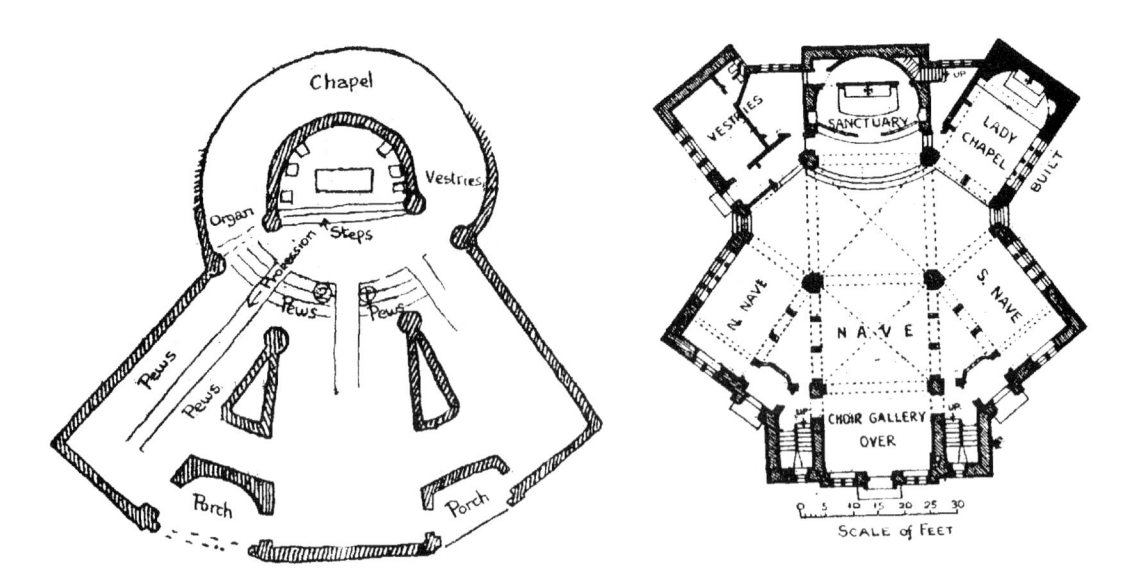

Original sketch and architect's drawing of St Luke's, Milber.

meant that the altar was visible to every member of the congregation, who could also see each other through the side pillars. Arthur Martin was intrigued by the design: after considerable research he was unable to find any record of a church of similar design, but he thought it was a feasible proposition, and drew up an initial plan. Keble produced this drawing at a meeting of the Church Council, and because only one or two people in Milber knew about the dream, it was assumed that the plan was his brother's design. They were delighted with it, and Arthur Martin was commissioned to establish copyright and reserve the design for Milber, a request that was hardly practicable.

Publication of the plan in *The Times* on May 3rd 1933, produced intense interest, both at home and abroad, and letters came from as far afield as Canada and Turkey. The article described the design as a 'bold experiment:'

An unusual plan has been adopted for the new church at the Milber Housing Estate, near Newton Abbot. Preliminary sketch plans have, in spite of its strangeness, been provisionally approved by both the Exeter Diocesan Advisory Board and the Ecclesiastical Commissioners, and the possibilities which the design opens up are well worth considering.

The plan is a complete departure from the basilican and cruciform types, to one or other of which most churches in Christendom belong, for there are three naves. These naves converge into a hexagonal central space on the far (or eastern) side of which there is an apsidal apse or sanctuary. The altar thus forms the focus point of each nave and is in full view of all the seats in the church. The three naves are not unduly isolated from one another, for there are open double arcades between them, allowing a view right across the church. The threatened difficulty of the effect outside of three converging naves has been well overcome by the architect, Mr Arthur C. Martin, FRIBA, as the sketch of the exterior shows.

There is no chancel. Many clergy would regret this, for there is often a strong sentimental attachment to chancels. But some will agree that the chancel is but a relic of the monastic foundation. Its omission brings the congregation nearer the sanctuary and altar, and makes the choir much more part of the congregation and the congregation part of the choir.

The triangular spaces between the naves will have low, flat roofs allowing clerestory windows to the central nave to be placed above them. Apart from the practical considerations, the plan makes what will certainly be an interesting and beautiful building in which scale and proportion can play their proper part.

Keble responded to this letter on May 5th, and took the opportunity to add an appeal for funds. His letter shows that he had a clear grasp of the financial figures, as well as the prospective development of the area:

Sir,

We would like to add a word of explanation to what was said in your issue of May 3rd about the design for a church at Milber. This is part of the urban district of Newton Abbot, but is in the ecclesiastical parish of Combe-in-Teignhead, and has been worked lately as a conventional district.

There are many families of railwaymen in the district, and no wealthy people. But there is a keen circle of Church life growing up, and during the last 4½ years, in spite of the hard times, about £960 has been raised for church building. Three years ago a mission building, with a small sanctuary was erected, and a prominent site has been secured for the church. The mission building is used as a Sunday school and for all social purposes and institute. For Sundays and holy days it has to be converted into a church and made fit for worship.

The cost of this building and of the church site have been paid off, leaving about £50 in hand towards the permanent church. This church, complete and furnished, will cost nearly £10,000. We believe it will somehow be built, but even if incomplete for a time, it would be a place reserved for worship.

The district hopes to be placed some day under the Diocesan Board of Patronage, and to be able to preserve its present custom of simple but dignified ceremonial. There is also a great wish to maintain a strong tradition of Church life. The work was begun early, and was there to greet many of the new residents when they arrived. There will be attractive building land around the church for at least 2,000 or 3000 people. We invite all who would be interested in this unusual building to send a contribution to the Milber Church Fund, Midland Bank, Newton Abbot.

Yours faithfully,
W. Keble Martin, Rector of Haccombe.

Arthur always maintained that the design of the church seemed to dictate itself, as though there was some mystical quality about it. A particularly interesting coincidence

Above: *The foundation stone.*
Below: *The exterior of St Luke's, Milber, from the west.*

happened when the completed drawing was being compared with that of St Olave's, Mitcham, which Arthur Martin had also designed. Arthur thought that the Dream Church was short in comparison with St Olave's, and asked his draughtsman what were the overall measurements. The answer was '83 feet 4 inches.'

'So what is the overall width?' Arthur asked.

The draughtsman measured the distance from the outer angle of the north nave to the outer angle of the south nave, a figure that as can be seen from the plan, is not a designed measurement at all. '83 feet 4 inches' he replied.

'And the height from the foundations?' asked the architect.

A moment later the reply came back, '83 feet 4 inches. So it was found that, without being intentionally designed as such, 'the length and the breadth and the height of it are equal'. (Revelations xxi 16) This is all the more remarkable when one realises that 83 feet 4 inches is in fact 1,000 inches.

By 1932 both the two-acre site and the mission room were paid for, and the Church Council was able to look forward to the next project – a unique and exciting new church for the parish of Milber.

In 1934 Keble was to move to the parish of Torrington; the rector of Combe retired and the Rev. Christopher Read was appointed to Combe-with-Milber. The levelling of the site for the new church began and 25 volunteers from the congregation undertook to do the preparatory work on the foundations. Keble was invited to cut the first sod in the place where the Lady Chapel was to be. It must have been an extraordinary moment for him: the beginning of the realisation of his dream, with all the worries of fund-raising lying ahead.

The foundation stone for the Lady Chapel was laid by Keble on June 15th 1936, and a few days before Christmas that year the Bishop of Exeter came to dedicate Milber's first permanent church building. The Second World War put an end to any further fund-raising, but the population of Milber continued to expand and by the end of the war had increased from 300 to 1,000. During the 1950s it doubled again, and the need for a larger place of worship was urgent. In 1952 the south aisle was completed and dedicated on All Saints' Day, November 1st, thus doubling the seating accommodation. Milber was then made separate from Combe-in-Teignhead; The Rev. G. R. Waldron, who had been priest-in-charge of the whole parish was appointed to Milber Conventional District, and a new rector appointed to Combe.

The need to complete the church was paramount, quite apart from the natural wish to fulfil the dream. With building costs going up as fast as funds were raised, doubts were expressed that the church would ever be completed. As a gesture of faith in 1961 it was decided to take the plunge and complete the building. Keble's youngest brother Richard undertook to help with the fundraising and raised over £2,000 by his personal efforts. The act of faith was rewarded; generous grants totalling £15,700 were received from the Church Commissioners and another sizeable donation came from the Exeter Diocese as well as a number of gifts and legacies. The total cost of the church was approximately £45,000, a considerable increase on the original estimate of £14,000 over 30 years earlier.

Among the correspondence with the architect was a letter dated 17th December 1954 from May & May, quantity surveyors, detailing the costings of the last contract for Milber Church. The total paid to the builders was £3,879.1s.4d made up of

£3,854 1s. 4d. as building works, £25 as quantity surveyors fees. Also a letter from Arthur to Rev Geoffrey Waldon, The Rectory, Combe-in-Teignhead, in connection with the proposed vicarage:

> I have been through the estimates for the vicarage with the quantity surveyor, and I can suggest a number of items which might be omitted. They are as follows but the figure is very provisional. Suggested reductions:
>
> Swing house to face south-east and bring nearer
> road to save length of drains and surfaces.
> Omit sitting-room bay (£60).
> Omit porch (£55).
> Omit 11-inch wall and door at west end of hall
> and substitute arch as at east end (£12).
> Omit bookshelves in study (£18).
> Omit basins in bedrooms (£15).
> Omit fireplaces in bedrooms and substitute electric (£40).

The church was finally completed in 1963. It was consecrated on 15th June 1963, exactly 27 years after Keble laid the foundation stone. It was only the fourth new parish church to be dedicated in the Moreton Deanery in 400 years. Keble remained reluctant to talk about the dream, although the story had been given wide publicity. So modest was he that he would not allow his name to be engraved on the foundation stone until shortly before the consecration, although he had laid it 27 years previously.

Keble, by then an old man, and a well-known public figure in his own right, was present at the consecration; Arthur was sadly unwell and died only a few weeks later.

The church today stands high above the A380 outside Newton Abbot, where the tourist traffic edges its way towards Torbay. The outside with its conical copper-clad tower and rendered finish is reassuringly solid; there is no indication of the breath-taking, almost dream-like quality of the interior. The unusual perspectives of the three naves, linked by double arcades under groined vaulting give a feeling of space and light. White-painted walls and ceiling contrast with moulded granite pillars. There are no choir stalls, and no screen between the altar and the congregation; the gallery over the west door accommodates both choir and organ. The main windows are of plain glass, with the light falling on to rich woodblock flooring and rows of oak chairs fanning out and away from the altar.

On entering the church from the west porch the ceiling under the gallery is only eight feet high. It then jumps to a 23-foot groined vault with high nave windows, each with five arched lights. Over the central hexagonal space the vault rises again to 34 feet with tall single windows that flood the area with light. The effect is of height and grace and but also of intimacy, with the altar becoming the focal point of each nave and the priest able to see every member of his congregation. They then become the immediate worshippers, and the choir become part of the congregation. An article in the local paper at the time reads:

The interior of St Luke's, Milber, looking east. (R.H.G. Martin)

The interior of St Luke's, Milber, looking west.

The church is a delightful building filled with interest. In accordance with the dream it has three naves linked together by double arcades to form a single unit which has an indefinable completeness, particularly when viewed from before the altar.

The three naves radiating from the sanctuary enable every member of the congregation to obtain a clear view of the altar and to be comparatively close to it. There is no chancel and no pulpit.

The clean white of the walls is emphasized by a deep red carpet which runs through the church. The floor is made of highly polished wood blocks and there is under-floor heating.

Over the altar hangs the 400-year-old Italian lamp which was given to the church … the font, of classic simplicity, was presented by the Moreton Deanery.

One interesting feature of the design was that there was no pulpit in the new church. This led to some interesting correspondence in 1947 between a Mr Henry C. Richardson of Ashstead, Surrey and Arthur's brother Dick, who was honorary treasurer of the Milber Church Building Appeal. Dick sent the letter on to Arthur who replied as follows:

29th April 1947

Dear Sir,

You wrote to Mr R. H. Martin commenting on the surprising absence of a pulpit in the Dream Church. It was I who received the original letter about the dream, written within an hour of its occurrence. For this reason I am invited to answer the interesting point you make. The first words used in that letter were: I was preaching from the altar step, for there was no pulpit and no suitable place for one.

That was what was dreamed, and it can either be accepted as having some meaning, or much more easily rejected and thrown overboard as rubbish. Other experiences I have had in connection with the dream make me unwilling to reject the picture drawn merely because I cannot explain it.

Christ was, as you say, the greatest of all preachers, but his evangelistic sermons were preached in the open, on the mountain, by the Sea of Galilee, anywhere outside. He 'taught daily in the Temple' giving instruction, surrounded by a group of His followers. It is doubtful whether there was anything like a pulpit in the Temple. Even in the early Byzantine churches there were no pulpits. Pulpits are relatively modern things. I think the earliest known in England only go back to the 13th century. The Ambo in Byzantine churches was primarily a reading desk, not a pulpit. Pulpits became bigger and bigger as the sermon became of greater importance.

The Church is God's house, primarily a place where He is worshipped, a house of prayer and praise, and communion with Him. Is this a partial explanation? Has the sermon somewhat usurped the real function of the Church?

Interestingly, the English Heritage listing notes: 'pulpit of a later design, objected to by Arthur Martin, who designed a moveable lectern.' It goes on to say that the church is …

'remarkable for its interior quality and extraordinary centralised plan, which anticipates one of the principal characteristics of post-war planning.'

Among the church records at Milber is a tribute to Dick Martin, who died in 1963:

> It is with regret that we record the death of Richard Martin of Exmouth. Mr Martin was the brother of both Arthur Martin, the architect, and the Reverend W. Keble Martin. He was Treasurer of the Building Fund and by his enthusiastic industry made large sums for that Fund. Although illness prevented him attending the consecration of the church, he lived to know that the work that he had so faithfully supported was complete. We offer our sympathy to Mrs Martin and his family.

Many years later, when Keble achieved fame almost overnight with the publication of the *Flora*, a member of the congregation at Milber embroidered the priest's cope with flowers taken from the *Flora*. (Colour Plate 6)

It is not given to many to have a whole church standing as their memorial. On the foundation stone set into the wall of the Lady Chapel the names of the two brothers, the priest and the architect, are a reminder of the spiritual strength, hard work and determination that resulted in the church of St Luke at Milber.

TWO CHURCHES

In addition to St Luke's, Milber, Arthur Martin designed two other new churches, one in the leafy suburbs of Mitcham, in south-east London, the other among the tower blocks of Camberwell. Each is also unique, and each has the unmistakable stamp of the architect – the Byzantine-Romano profile, the spacious interiors, albeit with a feeling of intimacy create by cross-vaulting and domed ceilings. It is possible to know without being told that those three churches – and indeed Sandhurst Chapel – are the work of one man, whose life was devoted to designing buildings for the glory of God.

St Luke's, Milber, was the second of Arthur Martin's three churches. The first was St Olave's, Mitcham. In the early 1920s the existing parish of St Mark's served about 20 houses in a rural area stretching from the east side of Mitcham Common across to what is now London Road. By 1927 this had grown to about 600 homes and by 1930 the number had increased to nearly 2,200 homes with a population of 10,000 with further expansion predicted. In a situation similar to that at Milber, the existing parish was subdivided and the parish of St Olave's created.

According to legend the name of St Olave is said to be derived from Olaf, King of Norway, an ally of King Ethelred II, who in 1014 drove the Danish invaders back from London Bridge and the surrounding area of Southwark. A church was founded in his honour in Tooley Street, Southwark, close to the south end of London Bridge. It was the first of several London churches to be dedicated to St Olaf. Tooley Street is a corruption of Olaf: the 'T' being taken from the final letter of 'saint'.

The church in Tooley Street was closed in 1918 and subsequently demolished: from the proceeds of the sale the trustees contributed £7,000 towards the cost of the new church at Mitcham and donated the pulpit, font and two bells as a tangible link between the old St Olave's and the new.

Like Arthur Martin's other two churches the design of St Olave's is Byzantine Romanesque, at a time when the favoured style for ecclesiastical buildings was almost universally Gothic. Also like the others there is no east window; he felt strongly that an east window can blind the celebrant as well as the congregation. He did not hesitate to use modern materials, and the domes, barrel vaults and pillars are constructed in reinforced concrete. A drawing in the consecration booklet shows a Gothic-style screen across the entrance to the chancel. It seems unlikely that it was ever built; if it were it would have been completely out of keeping with the concept of the design.

Arthur Martin's own notes on the construction of the church were printed in the Official Souvenir of Consecration, dated January 17th 1931. They say a great deal about the character of the man himself, his innate modesty and insights and his fundamental Christian beliefs.

THE BUILDING OF ST OLAVE'S CHURCH
By the Architect

The material realization of St Olave's Church began on Tuesday, June 11th last year when the Bishop of Woolwich and the Vicar of St Olave's called at my office in Lincoln's Inn.

At that meeting we discussed the sort of church it was to be, and then it was that a church of the Byzantine type was first suggested I think by me. What was more important, however, was that I then learnt for the first time something of the hopes and aspirations of those for whom it was to be built. Later on I learned still more when I attended the meetings of the Parochial Church Council.

The plain fact is that an Architect's inspiration comes not so much from within himself as from outside. The inspiration originated with those who saw the need for the Church and had some sort of picture, undefined perhaps and hazy, of how its appearance should bear silent witness to the central facts of life. This was the inspiration behind our medieval Churches and Cathedrals, and it is truly said that Bishop Hugh built Lincoln and William of Wykeham built Winchester. Theirs was the ideal and the inspiration behind those great Cathedrals. The names of the architects are half forgotten, yet it was they who crystallized the ideals of others into solid stone construction. So St Olave's owes most to those whose insight into the hidden things of life conceived the possibilities.

The form of the Church departs from the medieval type completely, but it is a reversion in plan to the very early Churches of Asia Minor. The underlying motif is Byzantine yet the treatment of the domes and arches is unlike any individual Church of that date. What the medieval type depended on was partly for its beauty on upright lines, on narrowness and height and radiated both mystery and emotion, well suited to that simple thinking and superstitious age, St Olave's aims at breadth of outlook so characteristic of individual intelligence today that accepts the help of Science where Science helps; and forms its own opinions.

The Church as at present built, is calculated to seat 515 people including the Choir, but it is far from complete. Another bay is needed to complete the Nave and this will add a further 145 seats. Besides this extra bay to the Nave, there are various things to be built when funds allow. The first of these will be the Lady Chapel on the North side of the Chancel.

The Lady Chapel will greatly add to the architectural interest and appearance of the Church. The entrance to it will be obtained by opening out the arch behind the Font, while the low arcade opposite the organ will become a double open arcade separating the Lady Chapel from the Chancel. This will add an alternative way for Communicants returning from the Altar Rail.

Then the Tower at the end of the nave will complete the exterior and provide a proper home for the bell, weighing 19 cwts, from the old St Olave's in Southwark. The present porches are temporary, and that facing Middle Walk especially will need rebuilding in a much more commodious fashion.

The Church is built on clay and rarely have I seen ground in a more sticky condition than this site when excavation started. However the foundations are ample, going down 5'0" and 8'0" below the level of the ground and the walls spring from a heavy bed of concrete. The walls generally are of brick and 23" thick, though this varies somewhat owing to formation of surface panels both outside and inside. No fewer than 380,000 bricks have been used to build the Church. The roof and all the vaulting is of the most recent type of reinforced concrete. In this respect at least the Church is very modern. But the old builders would have used it had it been available, and if the great Church of Saint Sophia at Constantinople had had its dome reinforced it would not have given the anxiety it has.

The outline of the Church is simple – some may regard it as severe – but it must be borne in mind that the extra length and western tower will alter this considerably. Why should it not be severe in outline? It is only more like the outline of our lives.

The present Tower over the Central Dome is not the Real Tower, which will rise eventually at the end of the building to twice the height of the present church. The existing central portion of the roof, however, is 40 feet above the ground, and from the top there is a wonderful view over the neighbouring roofs of the hills that stand around London.

Largeness is always comparative, but spaciousness is not. It is a quality that a building either has or has not got, and is independent of its size. This spaciousness St Olave's surely has, but for those who value figures I give the measurements.

Length inside (as built)	104' 0"
Width across transepts	68' 0"
Width of Nave	45' 0"
Diameter of Dome	41' 0"
Height of Dome (inside)	33' 0'
Height of springing of Arches	12' 0"

These measurements are big by the standards of many of our ancient parish churches, but small by other standards. Eight St Olave's Churches could be put inside the dome of that great Church at Constantinople. Yet we can call St Olave's spacious. Are there not English parish churches two or three of which would go inside St Olave's?

The Church does not lie East and West. To have put it so would have made it crooked on the site. The point was discussed at our first meeting on the 11th June. The tradition of orientation is principally an English one and is by no means universal even here. So it was decided to abandon any attempt to twist the Church, and the axis of the Church is nearly North and South, the 'East End' being a little east of North.

Finally; may I point out one feature of the interior of the Church. Standing at the 'Western' door, study the lighting and the effect produced. The windows as you face the Altar are not in front of you, at least they do not catch and blind the eye. Yet the Church is light, and the Altar domes and piers are all somewhat mysteriously bright beyond one's expectations.

Now study the effect of this light upon the Arches, groins and vaults and notice the wonderful graduations of shading and reflected light revealed on the curving surfaces. These delicate graduations are not so striking as to thrust themselves upon

The arched ceiling of the chancel, St Olave's, Mitcham. (A. Stocker)

St Olave's, Mitcham, showing 'temporary' west wall.

the notice, and are often missed, until one sees a photograph which shows them beautifully. These delicately shaded surfaces will, to those who see them, rob the building of austereness, and add refinement equal to the most elaborate detail of a Gothic Church.

Today the feeling of spaciousness remains, and any suggestion of austerity is offset by the curved surfaces of the ceiling and the decorated capitals on the pillars. The straight run of the eye through the nave and chancel to the sanctuary is blocked by a second altar at the chancel steps.

Outside, the church has not been treated so well. The 'temporary' west wall is still in situ, and the keying of the bricks waiting for the new wall is plainly visible on the west corners. The planned porch and bell tower never materialised: instead a small unsympathetic 1970s porch looks more like a bus shelter than the entrance to a beautiful church, and is totally out of keeping with the church itself. The original porch on the south side, now disused, looks sadly neglected, and is in danger of being overwhelmed by the adjacent shrubbery. The setting of the church has been further damaged by the construction of a hall on the north side and a block of garages within a few feet of the east end.

ST LUKE'S CAMBERWELL

St Luke's stands defiantly among the housing estates north of Peckham Road in south-east London. The surrounding area does nothing for the dignity of the church, but regeneration is under way and ultimately the setting of the church should be greatly improved. The style is again Byzantine, the exterior angles and planes reminiscent of its sister church at Milber, and its red-brick similar to St Olave's. St Luke's was designed by Arthur Martin; the foundation stone is engraved LAUS DEO 1952. The church was completed in 1954 after his retirement by Milner and Craze. It replaced two nearby churches which were bomb-damaged in the Second World War.

The exterior in red brick is austere, although in design the lines are also similar to Milber, though larger, 'but with greater subtleties and refinements, showing that Martin continued to develop and improve his designs even into his late seventies. The interior has the same qualities of light and shade with a greater interplay of arches; spaces and columns'.[1]

The sacristy is again apsidal, with the transepts and nave set around a central dome. The three-bay nave has round arches and columns with cushion capitals. Above the aisles the windows, in groups of five, are divided by smaller columns of similar style. The altar (Colour Plate 7) has a high reredos with a tester, and on either side, within the apse, are windows with good modern glass. The Lady Chapel is approached through a double arch with narrow columns and has a distinctive mural on the east wall.

For all the problems that might be expected from such an area, the church attracts sizeable congregations and is free of vandalism and graffiti. The vicar has been known to say that on occasions his has been almost the only white face.

---

[1]Ann Stocker: 'Arthur Campbell Martin CVO FRIBA. THREE CHURCHES.' *Association for Studies in the Conservation of Historic Buildings,* Volume 21.

St Luke's, Camberwell, exterior. (A Stocker)

The designing of a church is a complex and growing process which changes and develops with the architect's experience and within the restrictions of money and position. Could it be that when Keble had the dream in March 1931, he was subconsciously influenced by the design of St Olave's, Mitcham, which had been completed by January 1931? It seems likely that his brother had discussed the plans with him, and possibly shown him the drawings or that he had visited the site during construction, If so, there is no mention of it in his autobiography.

Alternatively, was Arthur's interpretation of the dream influenced by the work he had carried out at St Olave's and by his preference for the Byzantine style of architecture?

Any conjectures along these lines can now only be speculative. It remains for us to appreciate and admire these three churches which are the inspiration of one man whose working life was dedicated to building for the glory of God.

LATER YEARS

When Keble and his family moved to the parish of Great Torrington in the spring of 1934, the building programme at Milber was hardly under way. Keble was a great pragmatist, but it must have been hard to leave Milber just when the Dream Church looked like becoming a reality.

However he soon found there was plenty of work for him at Torrington, as the assistant curate had just left, the bells were away being re-cast, and the money to pay for them had to be raised. There was little time for holidays and relaxation, and the *Flora* was once again on hold, although Keble did fit in a few drawings for the *Flora of Devon*.

Soon after he arrived in Torrington Keble recalls a serious tragedy that occurred in the town:

> Sydney House, a very large house in South Street was taken over by the Devon County Council as a boarding school for backward boys. I went there with some regularity for little services of instruction. And I left there my old army knapsack, full of hymn books. One evening when the boys were all in bed, the staff were having supper together. But one of them had been ironing: and had left an electric iron switched on in the ironing room. The house had been constructed with a large central hall open right up the roof with broad and beautiful oak staircases, and Galleries for access to the bedrooms. This proved a most dangerous construction. Presently smoke was pouring out from the door of the ironing room, immediately poisoning the atmosphere of all the stairs and galleries. Boys began coming down and at first were sent back by a teacher, not realising the seriousness of the situation. By the time the fire brigade arrived the situation was desperate. Most of the boys were got down, all but seven. Some of these had dived under their beds to get air. Bill Kelly (our good church verger) was the captain of the fire brigade. He entered top-floor windows at great risk from a fire escape, and brought down four or five boys, but all seven died of carbon-monoxide poisoning. The ruins of the building were a mass of great icicles in the morning. And in due course we had a truly sad funeral gathering.

When time permitted. Keble continued to collect botanical specimens. He moved in somewhat elevated botanical circles, and describes a conversation with the head botanist of the Natural History Museum, a Mr Wilmot. They were discussing a small fern, *Asplenium septentrionale,* which they had found in South Devon. The name *septentrionale* describes a plant of northern or sub-Arctic origins, an indication that the temperature in Devon was once much colder: the term global warming was not then in common use.

He was busy completing his work on the *Flora of Devon*, 'quite a serious big work' of 750 pages, promoted by the Devonshire Association. He was one of seven botanists contributing to the study, and he says 'it seemed to fall to the Vicar of Torrington to be the principal editor.' *The Flora of Devon* was published just before the beginning of the Second World War in 1939; only 500 copies were printed as paper was already restricted, so they became almost a collectors' item.

Some years earlier in 1928, Keble had been appointed a fellow of the Linnean Society and sometimes attended meetings and exhibited drawings there. On May 23rd 1938 he attended the 150th anniversary of the Society and reported the events in the Parish Magazine:

> It has been the writer's privilege this week to attend a long series of addresses describing some of the latest discoveries and conclusions of a dozen of the great biologists of Europe, drawn from nine different countries. If some of our members fancy that modern science is not compatible with the Christian faith, it may be of some help to them to be assured that this is not at all the case.

However any further work on the *Flora* that Keble had hoped to do was brought to an abrupt halt by the outbreak of war. A battalion was billeted in the village and there was an influx of evacuees from Bristol into the parish, with the vicar and his wife constantly in demand for help and advice and the vicarage stretched to the limit. There were several weddings in the village, including that of his daughter Lisette. For a lot of the time Keble was working alone. He found there was not enough time for private study, and to his great distress he was obliged to preach 'almost in the words of sermons I had preached there already'. Keble obviously attached great importance to the weekly sermon:

> Some people seem to think that a padre can preach a sermon just out of his head. We are not so clever. It is necessary to spend a lot of time in study, to learn all about the subject in order to make sermons and class teaching really instructive. I have never preached another man's sermon. Much weakness of faith today is surely due to people not knowing what has been in the deep experience of mankind in the past, recorded in the Scriptures, and so what may indeed be our own moving experience today, a personal loyalty, which we check upon at the end of each day by self-examination.

By 1943, after ten exacting and tiring years, Keble felt he had 'delivered his message' at Torrington and accepted an invitation to return to Combe-in-Teignhead with Milber, where the progress of the new church had been painfully slow. The messages coming from the parish were that some people were saying: 'We cannot build the houses and we cannot build the Church. That Martin started the Church here and the Church will never be needed.' Keble felt that he was at least in part responsible for the situation there, and he thought he ought to go and 'bear the brunt of the supposed difficulties'. As he had never been Vicar there, only a voluntary curate, there was no reason why he should not return to work in the parish.

Almost the first thing he did was to apply for a permit for an auto-cycle: they had to wait seven months for it, but it proved to be a great help, as it 'went up those two steep hills at the same pace as it went down, and carried the Vicar often three times a day to and fro for visiting and for meetings'. As Keble was by then well into his sixties, he can be forgiven for requiring some help with the steep hills.

In spite of the rigours of war, Keble's enthusiasm for matters botanical was undiminished. He was also ahead of his time in other respects: he was involved with a group called the Nature Reserves Investigation Committee, a forerunner of the major conservation groups of today. This committee suggested that two large moorland areas should become National Parks, four smaller ones Local reserves, and that seven areas should become Amenity Reserves. This is similar to the system for the protection of wildlife and habitats with which we are all familiar today.

Together with their parishioners, Keble and his wife maintained steady progress with the fund-raising for the church. There were other restrictions familiar to anyone who remembers the war. Keble describes it with his usual understatement as 'the usual difficulties. It was all work. No service after dark at Combe owing to the blackout. No organist at Combe owing to military service.'

With the end of the war, work on the *Flora* was resumed, within the restrictions of finance and petrol shortages. In the severe winter weather of 1947 the steep hills were almost impassable, and travelling on the auto-cycle unbearably cold in the difficult conditions. Keble felt he could not risk the dangers of another winter like that one, so in 1949 at the age of 72 he resigned from his benefice. He and his wife Violet moved to a bungalow at Gidleigh, near Chagford, on the north-east edge of Dartmoor. He writes:

> I had resigned from my benefice, that is from my office as Vicar; but no man ordained a priest can possible resign from his priesthood. The rules of the Church are hard on those who resign their vicariate. They must live in a parish somewhere: but they are not allowed to be on the electoral roll of the parish or to have any voice or share in its Parochial Church meetings. The Rector of Gidleigh was very kind and allowed me to be in his choir and to read the lessons sometimes at matins or evensong. When we moved to Gidleigh I was put on a list called 'Special Service Clergy', and was posted by its secretary to any parish needing help. And when I had done some thirty weekends of services and visiting, I was licensed in the Cathedral by Bishop Robert Mortimer as a Public Preacher.

Keble derived great pleasure from his 'locum' work, standing in for the clergy in about 46 different churches during illness or holidays, and filling in between one vicar and the next in seven parishes. This was in addition to taking services at Gidleigh for 14 months during the Rector's illness and after his death. He was paid a travelling allowance of 6d per mile and a guinea a time for Sunday services, but of course parish visiting, which he had always so much enjoyed was unpaid. It had its own reward, as Keble remarked, he was relieved of the administration duties of a parish, and had the 'pleasure and privilege of talking sincerely to our fellow men and sharing with them the joy of Christian life'.

With more leisure time than when he held a benefice, the *Flora* advanced rapidly. Twenty plates were retraced and repainted, adjusting the position of the figures on the

SO RUNS MY DREAM

Family photo, 1952. Arthur is fourth from the right, back row with Hope on his left, then Keble. Keble's wife Violet is third from the right, front row.

page to improve the spacing. Some 200 further specimens were received from other botanists, either a new specimen or one from which he was able to improve an existing drawing. He had time to visit the Natural History Museum and the Herbarium at Kew for comparison of specimens and for adding those he had not been able to obtain.

Towards the end of 1957, when Keble had passed his 80th birthday, he and Violet realised that it was time to move again. From where they lived at Gidleigh, the church was half a mile away and some 200 feet uphill. He says, 'we needed, in our advancing age, to be able to walk into the local church easily, not puffing and blowing.'
Having failed to find a more suitable bungalow, they decided on a possible site where they could have one built. The price of the site and the design of the bungalow were agreed with the landowner, but as it was adjacent to the church, the patron of the benefice had some rights over it. He objected to a small house being built close to the church, so Keble and his wife went personally to ask his consent.

'No!' the patron replied. 'You may be a very nice man but you will very soon be dead, and your successor may be a horrid man.' Keble notes, with wry humour, that the patron himself did not live long after his firm refusal.

Finally they settled on a site at Woodbury, where a contractor was to build new bungalows near the church. But before they were able to move Keble's wife Violet suffered her first stroke. The move to Woodbury, however, went ahead, although a couple of years later the new bungalow was to prove a mixed blessing. A cloudburst on Woodbury Common flooded the little stream that ran along the bottom of the garden, as well as the sewers. Three manhole covers were lifted and the water poured out all over the garden. Then an enormous trench opened at the bottom of the garden, and the herbaceous border in full autumn colour was swept away, taking the rose pergola and a wooden fence with it. The contractors who had built the bungalow carried out the repairs, which were partly covered by insurance.

Further downstream was the little cob and thatch church at Exton, a daughter church to Woodbury, where Keble often took services. The cob walls were completely washed away by the flood, and the thatched roof collapsed to the ground. Many of the fittings were rescued, and an altar candle was later found under the railway bridge by the Exe estuary. This little church was in due course repaired, and Keble continued to take services there for a number of years.

In 1959 Keble and Violet celebrated 50 years of marriage, a joyful occasion for all the family. But the following years were less happy; their eldest daughter Barbara had been diagnosed with leukaemia and died in November 1960, having been to Keble 'a good intimate friend and a very dear eldest daughter'. Then in 1963 Keble lost two brothers: Arthur, his closest brother, and also a friend and colleague, died in June that year, just missing the consecration of St Luke's, Milber, which he would so much have enjoyed; and Dick, the youngest of the 'nine', who had worked so hard as treasurer of the building fund, died shortly afterwards. A short time later Violet, whose health had been deteriorating, died suddenly while in a wheel chair in the garden at Woodbury with her husband and two daughters. A tribute to her appeared in the Milber Parish Magazine of October 1963:

> On September 16th Violet Martin was laid to her rest in the churchyard at Powderham. Mrs Martin will be well remembered in the Parish as the founder of our

branch of the Mothers' Union, and for her other work which a parson's wife is called upon to do. Throughout her married life Mrs Martin was a handmaid of the Church and a source of inspiration to her husband. We offer our deep sympathy to the Reverend W. Keble Martin and members of his family.

Keble, then aged 86, was devastated by the loss of his closest companion, who had worked beside him loyally for over 50 years. With a husband who was frequently 'on another planet,' she had loyally and willingly borne the burden of family life. Keble writes:

My own home life became forlorn. I wished for more friendly companionship. The two things that helped to keep me going were the church work and the flower painting. I was doing all I could at both of these. They were like the two hand rails that we have in our bungalow, helping to keep old folk steady.

THE FLORA

With more time to himself Keble was able to give his full attention to the *Flora*, which was nearing completion. The time had come to find a publisher for Keble's lifetime's work, but this was proving difficult. The cost of reproducing high-quality plates was prohibitive, and those publishers that had been approached felt that the resulting high cost of the book would make it hard to sell.

In January 1959 Keble's coloured drawings had been exhibited at the Royal Horticultural meeting in Vincent Square. The president was then the Hon. Sir David Bowes-Lyon, and he was one of the first to sign an appeal for their publication.

Botanical correspondents were still sending Keble specimens of the rarer species which were on the 'desiderata' lists. Over the half century when Keble was working on the *Flora*, 82 botanists had sent a total of 360 specimens, an indication of the efficiency of the botanists network long before the days of the Internet. One of the difficulties he had to contend with was that the International Botanical Congress, whose Nomenclature Committee had been meeting for years to agree on international botanical names for species of flora, had come up with their findings. The result was that Keble had to wash out more than 200 scientific names and replace them with the amended ones.

In March 1961 Keble went to London specially to get signatories to an appeal for publication funds. Those prepared to support him included the two heads of the Botany department at the Natural History Museum: the Director and the Scientific Officer of the Royal Botanic Gardens at Kew, and a former Director of Kew, Dr W. S. Bristowe. He had been writing to Keble on the subject of publication since 1954.

The family were also doing their bit. Keble's son Patrick had sent out letters and appeals to 250 selected people and collected almost £1,000 from a large number of subscribers. His wife also wrote an appeal to His Royal Highness the Duke of Edinburgh, who asked to see some of the plates.

Meanwhile Keble, alone in the bungalow at Woodbury, and needing some help with his domestic arrangements, heard of a Mrs Florence Lewis, a widow, who had recently been helping to care for a friend who had died of cancer. She needed a change of scene, and she thought that looking after an elderly clergyman in South Devon would be just the job, as she had friends and relations in the area.

Keble found her pleasant and helpful and a good cook. A local volunteer who had been driving Keble to take the services at Exton church sold her car to Mrs Lewis, who was then able to drive him to church and on small outings. Keble reports that 'our mutual behaviour was polite and excellent, quite above reproach.'

By the summer of 1964, 33 of Keble's colour plates had been with Buckingham Palace for a year. When he wrote to ask when they could expect to hear, he was told that the previous day the plates had been taken to a meeting of the directors of Ebury Press, who agreed that they were just what they wanted. There followed many months of hard work, discussions and corrections on what was to be called *The Concise British Flora in Colour*.

The events of that year were described in an article by the editor, John Hadfield, in an extract from The *Bookseller* of January 1965.

FLOWERS FOR THE PRINCE

Publishers find MSS and ideas for books in all sorts of unlikely places. The mythology of the book trade is rich in the discovery of pencil-filled exercise books in farm cottages or lunatic asylums; chance encounters with literate taxi-drivers and gypsies, unforeseen meetings on the Great Barrier Reef or in Ronnie Scott's Jazz Club. I doubt, however, whether any publisher has picked up what now appears to be a readymade best-seller in the august environment where I found one a few months ago.

Let us look at this unusual event first of all from the author-artist's point of view. William Keble Martin, a schoolmaster's son, was born in 1877. In his schooldays at Marlborough he began to collect 'bugs' – as many schoolboys do. His study of the feeding habits of *Lepidoptera* led him to the study of plants. As an undergraduate at Christ Church, Oxford, he took botany as a subject for his degree, and as a student he was exhorted by his teachers to draw plants under a microscope.

In due course Mr Martin was ordained. For eighteen years he ministered in industrial parishes in the North of England. For a year during the First World War he was a chaplain to the forces in France. From 1921 for many years he had parishes in North and South Devon.

During the whole of this long period Mr Martin seldom had more than four or five days' holiday at a time. But every moment of leisure was devoted to the drawing and study of wild flowers. After a busy Sunday he would catch a midnight train to the habitat of some rare plant – in Scotland it might be, or Wales. Some of the flowers he picked had to be drawn as they faded in the train on the return journey during Thursday nights. Never did he draw any plants except from life.

Mr Martin was an active member of the two Botanical Exchange Clubs and of the International Botanical Congress held in 1930. He has been a Fellow of the Linnean Society since 1928. In 1939 he edited the 780-page *Flora of Devon*. He has a number of botanical coups to his credit, such as telling his fellow-botanists where to find the orchid *Listera cordata*, which everyone maintained to be extinct. Mr Martin had seen it forty years previously in Lank Combe. He conducted a party straight to the place he remembered, and there the orchid was still found to be growing, hidden under bracken.

After sixty years of study and research, when the last gaps in his drawing books had been filled, a representative British Flora had been compiled, with 1,400 different meticulously drawn in colour, in exquisite groupings: on a hundred sheets of drawing paper, uniform in size. To accompany these Mr Martin had written a succinct but botanically accurate text.

It had all been a labour of love – a leisure pursuit of a kind to which parish priests in Britain – as witness Gilbert White of Selborne – have traditionally devoted themselves. Quite naturally, however, Keble Martin wanted to get his *Flora* published.

Now we come to the publishing aspect of the story. Mr Martin's work was offered to seven publishers. All of them expressed great admiration for the work. All of them flinched from the large cost that colour reproduction involved. The general view was that it would have to be a five-guinea book, and it was doubted whether the market, at that price, was large enough to absorb an economic edition. One firm very nearly committed itself to the venture, but a change of directorship caused it to be abandoned.

Mr Martin, now retired from his ministry, was prepared to accept the fact that his life work would never be published. He made arrangements for all his drawings to be deposited after his death in the Natural History Museum, for the use of students.

His family and friends, however, decided to launch an appeal for funds with which to subsidise publication. £5,000, they had been told, would be needed to make it a viable publishing project. A number of botanists had responded, but nothing like the necessary amount had been raised when one day Mr Martin's daughter-in-law, reading about the Duke of Edinburgh's interest in natural history sent a copy of the appeal to him.

Prince Philip asked to see some of the drawings and was deeply impressed by them. As a result of the Duke's interest, which had been communicated to Robert Lusty of Hutchinson's, I went along to look at the drawings. Much as he admired them, Lusty felt they were not quite in Hutchinson's field of publishing.

When I returned to my office from Buckingham Palace, I found my colleague George Rainbird in conference with Marcus Morris, of the Ebury Press, and Peter Hebdon of Michael Joseph, who distribute Ebury Press books.

I put Mr Martin's drawings down on the boardroom table and said, 'I've just been offered these.' All three men were intensely interested – in the drawings themselves, I must emphasize; I mentioned their provenance, of course. But there was no suggestion at this stage that Prince Philip would write a foreword to the book.

That evening George Rainbird sat up studying the drawings with extreme care – he had a particular interest in botanical draughtsmanship – and working out a production plan. The next day the drawings were in the hands of Peter Jarrold of Norwich. Within a week Jarrold's had produced colour proofs of two plates and an estimate for printing 50,000 copies by tour-effect offset litho. Within another week a contract had been signed with Reverend Keble Martin for the publication of the book on a royalty basis. Within another week Marcus Morris and Peter Hebdon had agreed to put a 50,000 edition of *The Concise British Flora in Colour* on the market in May at a price of 35 shillings.

For the 87-year-old artist-author it was indeed a transformation scene.

I take no credit whatsoever for my part as a mere messenger in this play with a happy ending. It was George Rainbird who first saw that the previous publishers had been mistaken in viewing the project as one for a limited market at a high price. He knew that by the use of Jarrold's latest type of Vario-Klischograph electronic engraver a superlative job of colour reproduction could be done in a large edition at a relatively low price. The technical processes are Greek to me, but I understand that the original artwork is scanned by this electronic device, the screen positive being cut on to a plastic foil, and any necessary colour corrections are done at the same time. A contact positive is made from this plastic foil. If any small amount of correction is needed after proofing, handwork is used to give the last refinements of correction.

Top marks, therefore, to Jarrold's for being technically on top of their job. Top marks too to Marcus Morris and Peter Hebdon for not funking a 50,00 first printing.

And although I have been told that this is something I should not comment on, I cannot help referring, in a purely personal capacity, to the part which the Duke of Edinburgh played in enabling this sixty-years-in-the-making labour of love to find its way into print. How easy it would have been for him, receiving a letter from a complete stranger, merely to send back a polite encouraging letter. Instead, Prince Philip asked to see the specimens. Having seen the specimens, he took action. The results will be in the bookshops on May 10th.

There is a tendency for certain organs of opinion to assume that the Royal Family is not particularly concerned with cultural matters. Why this view should be given currency I cannot imagine. Queen Mary was intensely interested in the arts. The Queen Mother is well versed in both music and painting. It is not perhaps generally known that the Queen and Prince Philip in recent years have been making a collection of paintings by living English artists. And Prince Philip, as we know, is President of the National Book League.

This recent example of His Royal Highness' intellectual alertness and practical concern for the arts is surely significant. It also provides a fairy-tale ending to a lifetime of dedication to science and art[1].

Meanwhile Keble's personal life had taken a turn for the better. Although his polite and reserved attitude towards Mrs Lewis was irreproachable, Keble found he was depending on her increasingly. Like most men of his generation he was not domesticated, although his daughter recalls that he could at a pinch make porridge, a skill acquired perhaps on their camping holidays. On October 26th 1964 he suddenly proposed to her, to which her response was: 'Oh no, I like the name Lewis. Besides I should be ruined.' Keble assumed this to mean financially, as Mrs Lewis would give up her pension by marrying Keble. So their relationship resumed with total decorum: occasionally Mrs Lewis asked him if he regretted what he had said, to which he always replied, 'No, not at all.'

However on December 5th that year, the day that they heard from Mr Rainbird that the Duke of Edinburgh had agreed to write the foreword to *The Concise British Flora in Colour*, they were both so overcome by excitement that they fell into each others arms. Mrs Lewis consented to become his wife, and the date for the wedding was later fixed for January 27th 1965.

So the 88-year-old married his bride. The wedding took place in Powderham Church, with a family gathering at his daughter Lisette's house. Keble managed not to lose the wedding ring this time, and from that day Florence was known appropriately as Flora by the Martin family.

---

[1] Reproduced by kind permission of The *Bookseller*.

PUBLICATION

The date of publication for *The Concise British Flora* was drawing near, and the publicity machinery took Keble by surprise:

The British Broadcasting Corporation seemed to foresee its popularity. And in the daffodil time of spring Mr Kenneth Allsop and some assistants came to Broadymead, Woodbury for a whole day, taking photographs and getting conversation out of us to make a film. So on 6th April we rather unwillingly appeared in a television programme called 'Tonight'. I told some of these photographers that I had never been able to afford either the time or the money for television, and was never likely to be able to do so. Watching it seems to be just doing nothing for anybody. But it probably increased the sale of *The Concise British Flora*. And Mr Kenneth Allsop was very kind about it.

In early May that year they went to London. George Rainbird had produced a large library edition of the *Flora* and presented them with a copy as well as copies for each of their children. The book was printed on hand-made paper, made only in the spring and bound in white leather stamped with tiny blue flowers from the Auvergne region of France. Then they were granted an audience with His Royal Highness Prince Philip in order to present him with a copy and to get his signature to their copy. Keble writes:

This was on May 6th at Buckingham Palace, and was a happy occasion. It was at twelve noon, just at the time of the Changing of the Guard, the band of the Welsh Guards striking up just as we arrived. His Royal Highness was very kind, and was enquiring after a smaller edition, which could be carried on walks, and so make the expeditions of young people more interesting. After this Mr and Mrs Rainbird kindly entertained us to luncheon, then took us to the Lime Grove Studio to see a repeat of the television interview at Woodbury, which Mr Rainbird had missed.

It is not difficult to imagine the thrill this must have been for the modest and unassuming vicar from Devon. He seems to have handled the publicity with his usual courtesy and humility, and his new wife was more than equal to keeping the press at bay. When an interview for the *Readers Digest* went on for longer than she thought was necessary she quietly turned off the electricity, pretending there was an inconvenient power-cut.

The Concise British Flora in Colour (Colour Plate 8) was published on May 10th 1965. Over the following months Keble received letters from friends in all the places where he had worked during his long ministry, including people he had christened in his first parish, and small boys he had persuaded to join the church choir more than fifty years before, who were by then grandfathers themselves.

The following January they were invited by the booksellers Hatchards to attend a reception on the Martini Terrace on the sixteenth floor of New Zealand House. They stayed in a London hotel for 'this great event' and enjoyed the spectacular views over London. On arrival at the reception they were interviewed by a television film crew, and Keble later heard that the film had been shown as far away as New Zealand.

Keble Martin was by now a household name, although there was a comment in the press that 'booksey' success was not likely to spoil him. It was one of his great joys that the book was available in school libraries and therefore accessible to children. *The Concise British Flora in Colour* was the *Times* bestseller for 1965; with 100,000 copies sold in the first year and Keble was named Author of the Year. Hearing about the numbers sold, a doctor working in an isolated location in Australia wrote to Keble that 'there was some hope for humanity after all'. A parson in the South of England wrote in similar vein.

Keble was still taking Communion every Sunday, visiting parishioners and working in his garden. As ever, the visiting was closest to his heart, and he once commented that if the parishioner had the television on, the Vicar was quite capable of absentmindedly standing in front of it.

The following year Keble was invited by Exeter University to attend their Degree Day and to receive the honorary degree of Doctor of Science, which was conferred on him by the Dowager Duchess of Devonshire. Before receiving his degree he told the assembled audience of students, parents and staff that his book had been published in several countries; it had been issued in special editions for Holland, Sweden and the United States, and he had heard it had even got as far as Mexico. Although he was a frail figure by then, he enjoyed seeing the young graduates passing before him to receive their degrees. After all, he was a mere 70 years older than most of them. (Colour Plate 9)

Throughout all this busy, happy period, full of visitors and correspondence, none of the publicity and excitement seems to have gone to Keble's head. Quite unaffected by the mantle of fame, he was still filling in as a clergyman when the need arose; he took a number of services at the little church of Exton, and he once said that he knew all the wild flowers on his way to church, their names and positions, and that they seemed to be talking to him about their struggle to grow.

On October 28th that year, after a celebration of Holy Communion at Exton, Keble heard some more good news from one of his parishioners:

I was suddenly informed that the Postmaster-General had said on the radio that he was asking me to paint some stamps with wild flower designs. I heard direct three days later. There were no wild flowers to paint at that season. But I had the advantage of being allowed by the publisher to adapt drawings from *The Concise British Flora*. The designs were to be completed by 12th December.... On some days the light was too weak for me to see the colours properly by 2pm. So we had to rise early and use the forenoon. The stamps were to be printed at Messrs Harrison's Stamp printing Works at High Wycombe. And Mr York, director of Harrison's, kindly invited us to visit the printing works. So we were shown all over that wonderful place by Mr Gray. This was rather a thrilling experience. My own designs were completed at Woodbury, and were dispatched to Messrs Harrison's to be completed with the addition of the Queen's head on 5 December.

*Photograph of Keble Martin taken for the
publication of his biography in 1968*

The following February Keble and Flora were invited by the Postmaster-General to a press conference and luncheon with him at the Post Office Tower. The revolving restaurant with its ever-changing bird's-eye view of London was a great thrill to Keble.

The stamps (Colour Plate 10) were issued on April 24th 1967, when Keble and Flora were away from home, but they had many requests to sign stamps and First Day Covers. Westward Television showed a queue of local boys calling at their house in Woodbury to have their stamps signed on the first day. The four 4d stamps depicted a variety of wild flowers in groups, adapted from the *Flora*: the hawthorn and bramble, morning glory and viper's bugloss, ox-eye daisy, coltsfoot and buttercup, and red campion and wood anemone. An interesting detail is that the drawing of the morning glory flower has been turned the opposite way to the illustration in the *Flora* so that it faces the Queen, as though nodding 'good morning' to the Sovereign.

The publication of *The Concise British Flora in Colour* was the culmination of Keble's lifelong passion for flowers, and his vast expertise on the subject. Few works of academic distinction achieve the status of best-sellers. But few works of any kind combine such beauty with such usefulness and with such wide appeal to so many levels of knowledge and varieties of interest.

Keble celebrated his 90th birthday on July 9th that year; in the final chapter of his autobiography he writes:

> It is a curious feature of human nature that when one is known for something done, the people we visit are more willing to give attention to anything we say. If this happens we are surely responsible for making use of it.

Some years earlier Arthur had been suffering from failing health. He retired from his architectural career in 1952, by which time two of his assistants, Frank Whiffen and Cyril Pearson had each been with him for over 30 years. In a letter dated November 19th 1952 Frank Whiffen wrote to Hope:

> Your beautifully worded and well thought out letter to Pearson and self, about our beloved ACM's position has, as you were unconsciously aware, not taken us entirely by surprise. It has often been in my mind to tell him, especially in recent years, how much we have esteemed his placid, happy nature and how we have enjoyed working with him though all those trouble-free days, and on all sorts of intriguing and interesting schemes. You will possibly wonder why we have preferred to remain when tempting offers have been made for our services from outside sources, and when you say 'love, and personal service,' you have the answer.

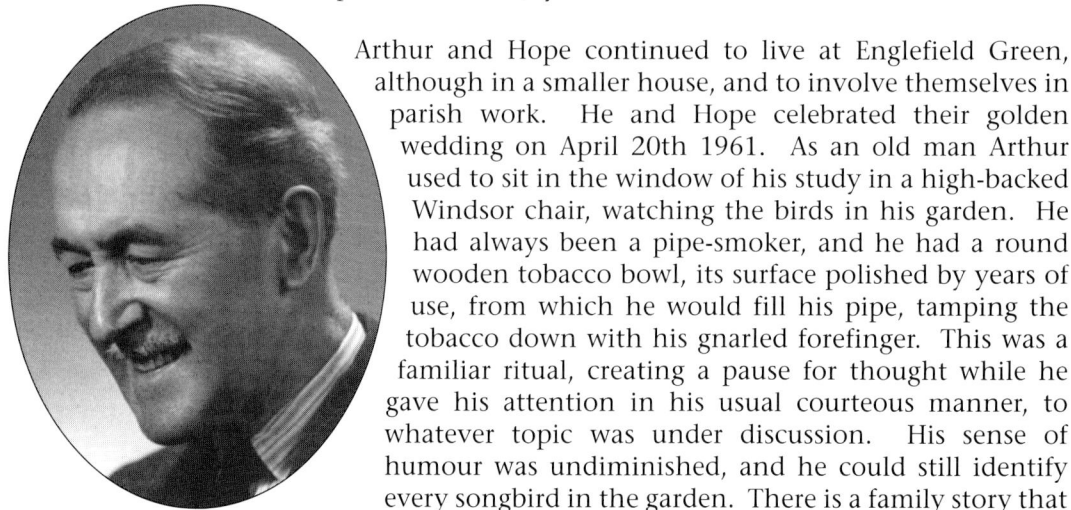

Arthur Martin on his retirement in 1952.

Arthur and Hope continued to live at Englefield Green, although in a smaller house, and to involve themselves in parish work. He and Hope celebrated their golden wedding on April 20th 1961. As an old man Arthur used to sit in the window of his study in a high-backed Windsor chair, watching the birds in his garden. He had always been a pipe-smoker, and he had a round wooden tobacco bowl, its surface polished by years of use, from which he would fill his pipe, tamping the tobacco down with his gnarled forefinger. This was a familiar ritual, creating a pause for thought while he gave his attention in his usual courteous manner, to whatever topic was under discussion. His sense of humour was undiminished, and he could still identify every songbird in the garden. There is a family story that in their old age he and Hope used to derive great pleasure from reading A. A. Milne's *Winnie the Pooh*

Arthur Martin's Golden Wedding, 1961.

together, a confirmation of the theory that the best children's books were really written for adults.

Arthur died on July 2nd 1963, missing the consecration of St Luke's, Milber, by a matter of weeks. In the Englefield Green Parish Magazine the Reverend H. J. Vallins, who lived in the vicarage designed by Arthur, wrote:

> Arthur Martin spoke of himself on occasions as a pilgrim. It must be a great satisfaction to Mrs Martin and to members of his family that in his earthly pilgrimage, which is now over, he helped many of us on our way.

Arthur Martin's memorial in the churchyard at Dartington, Devon.

PUBLICATION

Keble Martin's memorial at Woodbury, Devon.

Arthur is buried in Dartington Cemetery in the same grave as his father. His brother Jack, Rector of Dartington from 1921-1939, who died in 1943 at the age of 69, is also buried at the same spot.

Keble continued to work as a parish priest with his usual humility and dedication. Not long before he died he once remarked: 'The Lord still has work for me to do.' He died at Woodbury on November 26th 1969 at the age of 92, by which time some 200,000 copies of the *Flora* had been sold. His memorial in Woodbury churchyard reads:

In Memory of William Keble Martin MA FLS DSc
Born 9th July 1877
Died 26th November 1969
He loved God all his life
And served him in the priesthood for 67 years, 1902 – 1969
Artist and author

His second wife Flora, who died in 1983, is buried under the same stone.

In the foreword to *Sketches for the Flora*, published after his death by Michael Joseph, the curator of the Watts Gallery, Wilfrid Blunt, recalls a colleague at Eton some 20 years previously who had asked if he might bring a friend, 'an elderly Devonshire clergyman who had painted some pictures of wild flowers' to see him. He entertained no great hope that he was about to be shown anything more than some rather amateurish sketches of the flowers that happened to grow in and around the parish. The amateurish sketches, however, turned out to be a virtually complete British flora, which was to become a national bestseller.

Sadly, after Keble's death the colour plates for the *Flora* were sold and the collection was broken up, some of the plates going abroad.

Both brothers shared a profound religious conviction coupled with strong principles and strength of character. They worked with conscientious dedication and without thought of reward, sharing a sense of deeper values; a life's labour of love pursued in a spirit of profound reverence for life and for the Creator of life.

Among Arthur's papers was a small cutting from David Scott-Blackhall's *As I See It*. The author was blind, but his words evidently struck a chord with Arthur:

Almost everything I believe in begins with caring. Consider this, that if the earth were the size of a pea, the moon would be a grain of rice, seven and a half inches away. The sun would be two and a half feet in diameter, eighty yards away. On that scale, the nearest star in the universe would be eleven thousand miles away. The earth is less than a grapestone in the celestial vineyard, but man belongs, eternally, and is not deserted, and will not be.

APPENDIX

The Dartmoor Diaries of Arthur C. Martin
1905–1910

CAMP 1905

PUPPERS HILL CAMP

1905

THIS CAMP WAS PITCHED ABOUT 1400 FEET ABOVE SEA LEVEL AND WAS INTENDED TO LAST FROM MONDAY TO SATURDAY.

THE FOLLOWING CONSTITUTED THE PARTY:- THE REV. J.S.MARTIN, THE REV. W.K.MARTIN, A.C.MARTIN, BOB CHAMPERNOWNE, EDWARD CHAMPERNOWNE AND W.A.MARTIN.

31 July, Monday.

We decided to rise at 7.0 a.m. in order to put the finishing touches to the packing, and get Ernest started with the cart about 7.30.

At 8.0 Arthur was still in bed and the cart was still at the door at 9.30. After Ernest had received advice from ten or eleven people who "really knew", he started about 9.35; he was to call at Meads, and also at Hood, at which places he doubtless received further good advice, besides the additional luggage.

Keble and Willy arranged the start one hour later and got off soon after half past eleven! Jack and Arthur followed; Arthur's bicycle was ornamental with a large pair of hob nail boots hung on in place of a lamp, while Jack was carrying 'inter alia' a rifle and a saucepan.

At Hayford farm, reached after pushing our bicycles nearly four miles up from Buckfastleigh, we interviewed the farmer's wife; and accompanied by a very dirty little boy, we threaded our way among the geese to a loft at the end of the farm where we deposited our bicycles. The good woman promised to put a padlock on the door but the place was so dirty (evidently being used as a feather store) that we felt sure that no one would venture in without good cause.

Half an hour later, about 1.45, we halted and had lunch all together on the moor above the farm. Hardly had we eaten our first sandwich when Jack thought it was going to rain, and made us start off again up the hill, in order to pitch the tent before the ground got wet.

On approaching the site, we saw a small cairn, which subsequenty proved to be our belongings, deposited in a heap on the open moor; and after driving off several inquisitive ponies we at once set to and pitched our tents.

Having made a good job of pitching our tents, we finished our sandwich lunch about 3.15 and shortly afterwards put on the kettle to boil for tea, unpacking meanwhile all the kitchen utensils. Our camp consisted of a regulation bell tent, purchased second-hand for 35/6, and the little calico tent, manufactured at home and used as our kitchen.

We had two paraffin lamps, which did not prove a success, owing perhaps to the subtle drafts of the open moor, they took an hour to bring a saucepan, and forty minutes to bring a kettle to the boil.

Tea was laid on the dry grass outside where it was fresh and sunny; Willy remarked that there were "millions of bugs on all the plates and things", to which Keble answered that "hay insects only tickle", so everyone felt re-assured.

The evening was spent in camp, arranging our goods and making up the many deficiencies of our kitchen tent. We even took the precaution to trench slightly on the upper side of the bell tent.

Then dinner was set to cook, but it was nearly nine o'clock before we started our first real meal in camp; everything seemed to take so long to arrange and so long to cook.

Just as dinner was ready, Edward arrived very hungry and admitted with the rest of us that he had never tasted anything so good.

After dinner we sat awhile and discussed the situation, before starting on the laborious process of washing up; this, like everything else, was done most beautifully and, before turning in, the kitchen tent was arranged with the greatest care in every detail, the lamps put out, and the door shut up for the night.

The bell tent door was soon shut after, and we were sampling our rather 'boney' patch of ground, that did duty for bedsteads, with mixed feelings; someone suggested it was "beastly hard".

The N.W. wind had dropped, and the night was still and dewy, not to say rather cold and, though sleep was rather fitful with most of us, the night was undisturbed till 2. a.m.

At that hour there was a thud; someone said "What's that?" in a frightened voice; then silence. Keble was next seen to put his head out of the tent, and sentry like to challenge an unseen enemy with "Who's that?" Then the flash of a lamp on the tent justified the question, and Bob's voice answered "I'm awfully sorry you chaps at turning up so late".

Bob had come across the moor by the light of a bicycle lamp, having left Torquay at 10 p.m. on a bicycle. He was soon accomodated with food and blankets, and the night resumed its peaceful aspect.

1st. August, Tuesday.

The day started early; Jack could not sleep after the great excitement of our midnight adventure and crept out at 4.30 a.m. with a fishing rod. He was followed by Willy, the rest of us sleeping on, in spite of whispered conversations, till 6.0 a.m.

Breakfast was ready about 8.30 and we spent the morning quietly about camp. The bathing pool was most delightful and refreshing, but only one member of the camp shaved during the day!

Rations were served for lunch, so that the party might go off each as he liked; and the bread having momentarily run short, Jack came off with a sandwich made of ham and dough cake.

The two Champs went off over Puppers Hill and brought back two small larch poles with which to strengthen the kitchen tent, which subsequently proved of great value.

Keble went off down the Avon valley in pursuit of botanical specimens. Jack and Arthur moved round the bell tent 45 degrees on account of the wind having changed to S.W. and they re-pitched the kitchen tent on the lee side.

Jack and Willy fished with great zeal and some success, with the result that we started dinner in the evening with fried trout; it may be said that Edward proved to have ideas (and possibly some experience) on the cooking which proved of no little value.

Tuesday night was again quiet, and after washing up we turned in about 11 p.m: the ground seemed to make most perfect beds, and we slept very soundly, in great contrast to the first night.

We found our feet met round the tent pole, but it only helped to keep them all warm. It was made a definite arrangement that each should turn over, stretch or otherwise kick the others ad lib. so no one had need to feel disturbed thereby. Everyone managed their beds and blankets better, too, than on the first night, and so felt the cold less.

2nd. August, Wednesday.

The camp was astir about 6.0 a.m., everyone feeling much the better for a good night's rest. The moor was glistening with dew in the bright morning sunshine; and the bathe, with the subsequent process of dressing in the open air, was most ideal.

Let it here be noted that quaker oats, and nicely cooked rashers of bacon, taste better on the moor, than anywhere else; breakfast, more perhaps than any other meal, proved that there lay dormant in several members of the party a great skill in the culinary art; and it is only to be regretted that owing to circumstances our meals took so long to prepare and clear away, for they were not long being eaten! Breakfast was laid, as on Tuesday, on the somewhat dewy grass outside the tent, and every member of the party had a different attitude for the meal. Jack upheld the dignity of his age by sitting on a basket, while the rest sat on the ground, squatting on waterproofs, down to Willy who lay at full length.

A long walk had been arranged, but after breakfast Jack and Keble, by previous arrangement, went up to the Warren House to christen the keepers youngest child, who was named Millicent Vera. The keeper and his wife (Mr. and Mrs. Pearce) were delightfully hospitable, and besides supplying us with milk and bread, were never failing in their readiness to help us to the utmost of their powers.

About 11 o'clock Arthur, Keble and Edward started off (nominally to Cut Hill) with sandwiches in their pockets, passing over Ryders Hill where the view was very fine, and from which the camp looked a small speck on the huge open moor, they made their way down to the Swincombe river, where they lunched. Then crossing the West Dart by the Prince Hall bridge, they made a straight line for Wistman's Wood leaving Two Bridges on their left. Several good plants of white Bell Heather were found, and Keble got some 'Autitrichia' moss off the oaks in Wistman's Wood, before they returned to Two Bridges for tea. The jam and cream were all- right.

Just before reaching Ryders Hill on the way back, the rain began, and in half an hour all three were wet through.

On reaching camp it was found that Jack had built a fireplace, and the blue peat smoke was being swept up the valley by a strong S.E. wind, accompanied by a drenching rain.

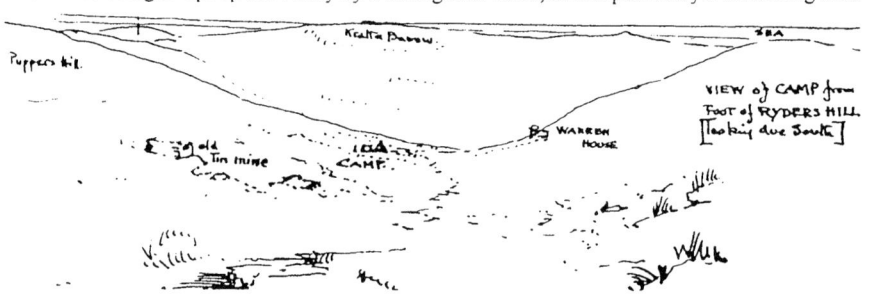

Meanwhile a slight accident occurred by which the camp nearly got burnt. In the middle of the day the kitchen tent was found to be quite black, likewise everything in it, from the flaring of one of the oil lamps. Soot hung everywhere, and much time and trouble was required before the place was put tidy.

During the evening the storm increased and every precaution had to be taken to prevent the tent being swept away. The kitchen tent was patched up and tethered in every direction before it was left for the night, and even then it was not expected to survive.

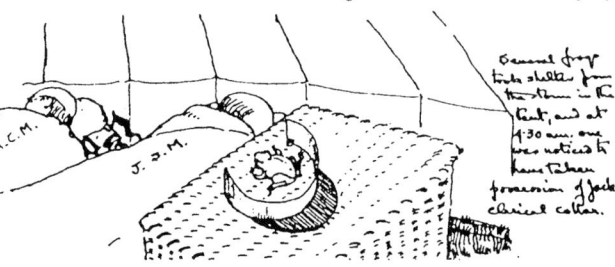

All night through the bell tent roared over our heads and the rain, driven by the gale, rattled like overhead thunder. The heavier storms came through the canvas in a fine spray and the windward side of the tent became uninhabitable; the mackintoshes covering the clothes on that side held pools of water in the morning. The pegs, driven as they were into rather peaty soil, were on our minds, so Bob with a minimum of clothing and a mackintosh took the heavy mallet, and put them out of sight and out of mind as he expressed it. It was a rather sleepless night for some, the noise being simply indescribable.

3rd. August, Thursday.

In the early hours of the morning Keble went for a run and shampoo in the wind and rain, and found that the kitchen tent was still standing.

Curiously enough as the wind and rain descended, the spirits of those in camp became boisterous too, and it would have required a phonograph to have recorded the many witty sayings.

Of course it was very important not to touch the inside of the tent for fear of the rain coming through, and it very much cramped our movements. Jack cruelly suggested, when one longish member clambered in, that there was "no room for a giraffe", and that he "had better be pegged into bed".

Theories too were rife on when the storm would cease; and Bob had one:- "The more the wind the less the rain, and the less the rain, the more the wind, you know what I mean!" "Yes" suggested another (who had had a good night) "I understand you mean - the more the less the wind the rain". So we wiled away the stormy hours of the morning.

The cricketing spirit of the party was in evidence; it was remarked that we were having an "innings" of uncommon fast "bowling"; and subsequently each fresh burst of the storm was styled a 'full pitch' or 'yorker' as the case might be, with intervals between for the bowler's run.

Whilst breakfast was cooking the whole party set to and drained the camp, digging a large outer trench right round both tents. The small trench round the bell tent had saved us from being swamped, but was quite inadequate. All the ground outside, and the ground inside the kitchen was sodden with water; and as we paddled round with bare feet and mackintoshes, the water was oozing up round our ankles. Inside the bell tent the ground was becoming decidedly damp and we completed our drainage system none too soon. The peat fireplace was 10 or 12 inches deep in water, and both cooking lamps had been swamped.

About 10 o'clock the gale moderated a little, and the day brightened so much that there were alternate showers and gleams of sunshine. The stream had risen during the night from a six inch bubbling brook to a torrent two feet deep and proportionately wide; yet Arthur and Willy both had some success with the fly, and there were trout to fry in the evening.

During the day Jack and Edward left for the Dartington Cottage Garden Show, which seriously broke the party, for as the day advanced the wind and rain increased, and they were unable to get back to camp.

In the evening we built a peat wall, about 3 feet high round the kitchen tent in the hope of saving it for another night and also took the precaution of having all breakable crockery, the milk, and other perishable articles in the big tent.

Mr. and Mrs. Pearce were quite solicitous for our welfare, and besides having very kindly dried a lot of our clothes, they lent us a large tarpaulin in the evening.

As darkness came down, so did the storm, and although there was perhaps less rain than the night before, the noise of the gale was fearful. It was very wonderful on these two stormy nights to note the contrast with the marvellous silence and stillness of Monday and Tuesday nights. During the gale the noise, even outside the camp, was past description; the wind howled over and round the rocks and through the heather, the rain hissed and stung; and then the tents roared in the wind, and the tightly strung ropes sang like violin strings. No member of the party will ever regret having witnessed such a scene.

As there were only four of us left, we all lay on the lee side of the tent, so there was no need to carry out Edward's suggestion of the previous night, that Bob should lie on his back and catch the drops in his mouth instead of getting wet.

We all four slept pretty well in spite of the difficulties, until the early morning.

Friday. August 4th.

About 5.30 we had a series of squalls worse than anything we had so far experienced; we all started up out of our sleep and watched the tent over us bending. The pole bent seriously all through the storm, which at once caused the canvas on the windward side to slacken and roar in the wind. The ropes were already dangerously tight though we dared not slacken them.

We had little hope of finding the kitchen tent standing, and agreed we ought to look for it on Ryders Hill two miles away.

The tent was standing however! but the back was blown out! Everything inside was of course swamped, and breakfast was cooked in the bell tent. The remains of the kitchen

THE CAMP at 7·0 am ON FRIDAY MORNING

tent were then rolled together, and laid on the ground. During breakfast we decided that another night would be too much of a good thing, unless the weather showed signs of real improvement; failing this, we decided to place our goods inside the bell tent, and set out on foot at 5 o'clock for home.

The whole morning was wet, the wind driving the rain and clouds up the valley with terrific force; it never lifted at all, and we could rarely see more than 100 yards.

We never required any artificial recreation, such as cards or games, even on this wet morning, for there was always lots to do or talk about.

About 1.30 when lunch had already been suggested, we were much pleased to see Jack returning to the camp. He had come up by Buckfastleigh on his bicycle, and had walked out over Puppers Hill in the storm; on leaving the wood at the foot of the hill he soon lost his way and was passing away on to the moor right above the camp when the clouds lifted momentarily and disclosed the camp half a mile away on his left, and turning back he safely reached us.

His news was that Ernest was actually on his way to the foot of Puppers Hill with the horse and cart, the home office having decided we had had enough. We packed up with all haste, despatching Keble to bring Ernest and the cart over the moor.

This proved no easy job for the moor with its rocks was not made for bringing carts over. They were also in a thick driving mist on top, so much indeed as to evoke the remark from Ernest that 'he would not like to have done the job without Mr. Keble'. But Mr. Keble proved a safe guide, and Ernest has added one more to his well assorted experiences.

We loaded up the cart, and settled up with the Pearces; and after we had had a good healthy slice of cake all round, we accompanied the cart on its rather perilous journey over the hill, getting off about 4.30 p.m.

THE LAST MEAL

We reached the lane by Hayford Farm at 5.20, took our bicycles out of the barn, and rode home, leaving Ernest to do the rest of the journey by himself.

CAMP 1906

1906 PUPPER'S HILL CAMP.

"Yes, its one of 'em" was the remark of our old friend, Mr. Pearce the Warrener, as Keble slowly climbed up to his house on July 18th. to arrange the preliminaries for the 1906 camp.

He found them little changed after 12 months and as ready as ever to provide milk and bread for a party of seven.

The following day, July 19th., Bob, Gilbert and Edward Champernowne came up and pitched their own tent, purchased like ours of Mr. Tope of Plymouth, on the old site.

Nothing seemed changed. Even the trenches we had dug in the storm of 1905 remained clean and fresh, as if they had been cut a week before.

It was not until the following Wednesday (25 July) that this advance party, after six days more or less in the clouds, were joined by the rest. "The rest" consisted of Jack, Arthur, Keble, and Dicky Fellows, the latter of Beeston fame, and "hereafter referred to" as "Dicky".

Wednesday, July 25th.

The start was effected by Ernest and the cart soon after 10 a.m., everything being most carefully arranged beforehand in the light of experience. So much discussion was there on the Tuesday evening, and so minutely were matters thought out, that it was discovered that no fewer than fourteen 'lists' had been made; it was even suggested that they should be catalogued.

The climb up from Buckfastleigh to Hayford Farm was terribly hot, and we all took off both coats and waistcoats, while horseflies tormented us, just as they had a year ago.

Ernest brought the Parsonage cart right over the moor from Cross Furze, piloted first by Keble and then by all four, the others going on to Hayford Farm to leave the bicycles.

HAYFORD GATE

The road ends here and the moor begins. It is an awkward spot, and it was here that the Champernowne cart was brought to a "full stop", their goods being transhipped to another cart above the gate.

The great difference between this years camp and last years is the second bell tent which the Champernownes had already got into working order, when we arrived.

We decided that the old site was not quite so good as another about 150 yds. down stream, and that much nearer the bathing pool. So we moved the Champernownes tent and pitched the two bell tents side by side, with the old kitchen tent, which Molly had sewn up, just behind them.

At this stage Gilbert inquired whether the camp stores from Hood had arrived; and the inquiry brought to light the first great defect in the preliminary arrangements, for it was discovered that nobody had told Ernest to call at Hood. This left us without any bacon, an 8 lb. leg of mutton, a beef steak pie and all our green vegetables.

We had hardly got the tents pitched when a party of four ladies arrived, our first visitors in camp. What they thought we don't know, but they had orders to get tea ready at once, and they did it. It was a long job as it was not until they had left that we got our fireplace built for the peat fire which, subsequently, did most of the cooking. The oil stoves were most useful but only as a slow fire for porridge and such like.

It was a beautiful day for starting the camp, the sun and wind having thoroughly dried the ground.

In the evening the wind dropped and the dew made the atmosphere rather chilly for supper which was laid, like all our meals, on a matchboard table out in the open.

The night fell with a cloudless sky and owing to a rather heavy day we all slept better than we expected.

Thursday, July 26th.

A heavy mist greeted us when we put our heads out about 6.30 a.m. and remained down till about 8 o'clock. The bathing pool would have been risky for anyone "with a heart", and with no sun it required some nerve to make the first plunge.

When the first bathe was over and one strolled back to camp, one appreciated to the full the scenery, the rolling mists on Kratta Barrow, the ferns and foxgloves, the Wheatears and Meadow Pipits, and lastly the blue peat smoke beyond the tents, a sure sign of a good breakfast to follow.

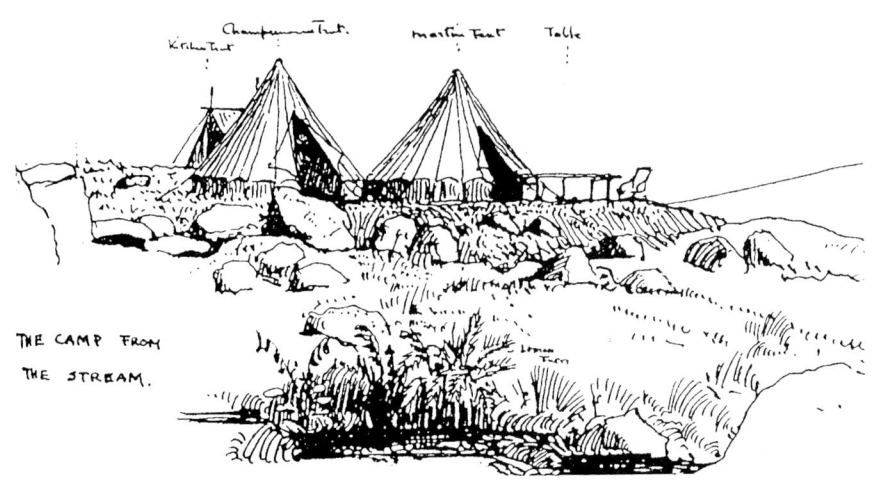

About eleven o'clock the post arrived, and a few minutes later a letter from

Elinor informed us that the Parsonage cart was at that moment due to arrive at Hayford Gate. Jack, Arthur, Bob and Edward were soon on their way thither, only to find that the cart had come up by Cross Furzes. They toiled back to camp in all the heat of a cloudless sky and the haze of an east wind to find that Ernest had arrived and deposited the Hood supplies and was starting back. Keble and Dicky had meanwhile gone up to Kratta Barrow, the party not collecting for lunch till nearly 2 o'clock.

In the afternoon several of the party took rods and went down stream to flog the water. They may have flogged it, but not successfully. One small trout was the day's catch, inspite of Edward's assertion that there were squads of fish in the river.

Supper in the evening got rather late, and it was ten o'clock before we had washed up.

Each evening we had Curlews and this evening we also noticed a pair of Ravens pass the camp, croaking in an unmistakable fashion.

Friday, July 17th.

The morning began for us at 6.15 with a heavily overcast sky, which cleared off between seven and eight. There was no doubt about our being in for a fine, hot, day.

We were rather late with breakfast and the subsequent clearing up, and it was eleven o'clock before Keble and Dicky were ready to start out on a long walk.

A preliminary parlance in the Martin tent had decided on a huge walk on Tuesday or Wednesday, starting at 5.0 a.m. and this decision modified Keble's and Dicky's walk in that it made a visit to Postbridge unnecessary, so they went to Hamel Down instead. Dicky dropped the belt of his Norfolk jacket when going out, and by a great coincidence found it on his way back not knowing where he had dropped it. Keble seemed to have had a good day for, in addition to a 20 mile walk and beautiful views, he had found some "asplenium lanceolatium", a rare fern.

Meanwhile, another coincidence happened. Arthur had been fishing with some success and when about to give up, caught his fly in a bit of bracken. On freeing it he found it also entangled in a cast and fly, which Gilbert had lost an hour or two before.

Supper in the evening was rather late but very acceptable; the plum pudding was especially appreciated. Jack had by this time entirely mastered the difficulties of a peat fire in the open, and little difficulty was found in keeping it in over night.

Saturday, July 28th.

The morning broke very dull and rather close. The bathing pool was quite a pleasant temperature, and by breakfast time the sun was shining and half a gale was blowing. Half a gale is entered tentatively for there was no small argument as to the strength of the wind, some putting it at 30 miles an hour and others at only twelve.

Two or three of the party went afishing in high spirits, and the same two or three returned peculiarly gloomy. Total bag recorded, one trout and 3 rabbits. Two of these rabbits fell to Edward, one to a gun shot, one to a rifle shot at the great range of 5½ yds! Jack made a record shot with his rifle and is backed for the King's Prize at Bisley next year. At about 30 yds. a rabbit's eye was seen blinking behind a tuft of grass and, no other part being visible, he aimed and hit that eye.

About 12.30 there was a scud of rain which soon turned into a heavy, driving, mist. Peter's Cross disappeared, Snowdon disappeared, Kratta was blotted out, and about 1.30 the

Warren House also vanished in the clouds.

We lunched. We discussed the weather. We played "pit" till everyone was hoarse; and then we had tea. It was as wet as it could stick; but the wind began to moderate and about half past five we put on mackintoshes and sallied forth.

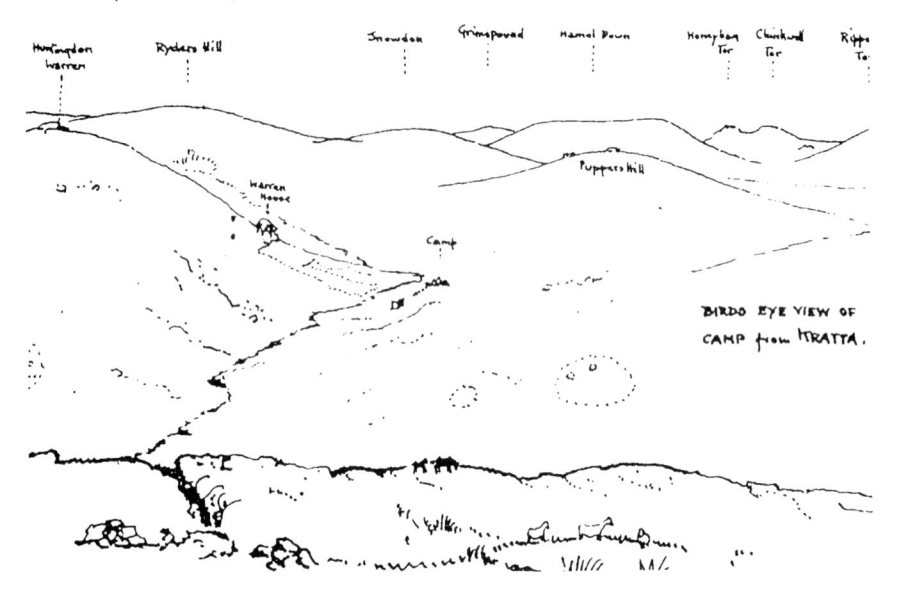

Some thought the trout would rise, and two of the party went down stream to try, but again they had no success.

Supper, like lunch and tea, was laid in the Champernowne tent the menu consisting of rabbit pie and pineapple 'chunks'. Supper was followed about 10 o'clock each evening by hot cocoa which, in the chilly night air, was most 'grateful comforting' and an excellent nightcap.

Sunday, 29th. July.

Sunday morning early was dull but, as usual, about breakfast time the clouds broke and it turned out a most beautiful day.

Unfortunately, Edward was seedy and Doctor Jack had an opportunity of experimenting on a fairly docile patient. And let it be at once said that in 24 hours the patient was the right way up again.

About half past eleven we adjourned to a rocky dell; and amongst the bracken and foxgloves and within hearing of the stream we had Matins. There was a gentle S.W. wind blowing and meadow pipits fluttered around in the most interesting way.

After lunch Keble suddenly informed the party, in an almost distressed tone of voice, that his bed was made of "Potentilla Tormentilla", Hyloconimum Squarrosum" and "Agrostis Alba". On further enquiry they proved to be a flower, a moss and a grass respectively.

The afternoon was spent quite lazily, tea seeming to come very soon after lunch, owing perhaps to an argument partly on scientific subjects, and partly on English Grammar. Curiously enough, English Grammar was a frequent source of difference of opinion. On

Saturday, for instance, the lunch argument was on the uses and abuses of the subjective mood!

MATINS CORNER

Evensong was held in the parlour of the Warren house, and Mr. and Mrs. Pearce and their eldest girl were present. It was a much more ambitious service than the one in the morning, for we sung the canticles, and had two hymns, all going very well. At the end Keble gave a short address which, although practically extempore, was very much appreciated.

After service Gilbert and Arthur went to the top of the Warren and Keble and Dicky to the top of Puppers Hill to get an appetite for supper and to fit them for an early retirement; in fact it was our earliest evening and we were turning in soon after 10 o'clock.

Monday, 30th. July.

During the night there was a heavy shower of rain, so much so that Keble got out and loosened both bell tents. This was followed by a very cold morning, making us all very restless and about 5.0 a.m. Jack took the mackintoshes off the pole, and threw one over each of us. This had the desired effect of making us warm and sleepy.

Keble was up soon after six and after a mouthful of "some'at to eat" he and Dicky started off down to Dartington to find out what the ladies were going to do, for they had been invited to tea at the camp.

Meanwhile, the camp had a good cleaning in preparation for our visitors, even the knives were polished, and the table cloth was washed by Gilbert in the stream.

At 12 o'clock Jack and Edward went off "just for a few minutes" with a rifle to see if they could bag a rabbit or two. They did not reappear again till after 2 o'clock.

Keble and Dick returned at 12.25 and, with Arthur, started off laden with lemons and lunch to Three Barrows where the ladies were going to have lunch, and brought them back to camp to tea. It was a good walk and a beautiful day. Several buzzards were seen and a

THE LADIES waiting for the lemons on THREE BARROWS.

young snipe was caught and, with some difficulty, photographed before it was allowed to go.

The ladies who came to tea were Miss Peak, Miss Fellows, and Nelly so that, with the seven of us, we sat down ten to tea. Not that there were ten seats, for three at least of us sat upon the ground. Our visitors thought they knew something about housekeeping, so they were politely invited to wash up, which they did with moderate dexterity.

They left at 5.45 to walk to Buckfastleigh, one of them shocking our sense of propriety by exclaiming "What a pestiferous nuisance, someone has nicked my painbox," meaning apparently "What a coincidence, I have mislaid my paintbox." Arthur and Keble saw them on their way, Keble entirely losing himself in a mist that settled down on his way home, and not arriving in camp till after nine o'clock.

Meanwhile, Dicky had been cooking the supper and had a slight accident with the broad beans. He was washing them by the stream in a cracked bowl when the bowl broke and the beans fell into the water. With great presence of mind he ran to the next waterfall and caught each bean as it came along and so recovered the whole lot and we ate them in due course.

The evening was misty, but the moon was now past her first quarter and gave splendid effects on the mist and hills around. So bright was it that Jack and Edward tried fishing with worms between 11.0 and 12.0 but without success.

It had been the longest and heaviest day we had had, and we turned in each at a different hour, but all equally exhausted.

Tuesday, 31st. July.

The night had unexpectedly turned wet, and about four in the morning, a heavy storm came right through the tents, and caused Arthur to hastily cover himself and his bedclothes with mackintoshes.

It was rather late, nearly 7 o'clock, when the camp began to stir, and the first man out found a wet drizzling morning.

We breakfasted in the Champernowne tent, and it was not till after 10 o'clock that the weather began to clear.

In the morning the postman, who only came three times a week, brought the post about 11 o'clock, and this included a packet of "Maxwells red and blue" flies. They seemed to turn the tide of bad luck for the fisherman, "floggers" as they were called; and Jack, Arthur, Gilbert and Edward all had some sport. Arthur and Edward both landed a very good fish (for the stream), regular "whales" as they remarked.

The afternoon turned hot, and the evening brought along the mist again, rolling over the tors down into the valleys in great billows glistening in the moonlight.

Supper was quite a "notable" meal, as Jack would say. We had a pie cooked by Mrs. Pearce and made of rabbits out of the heather, a dish of trout out of the stream and wortleberries off the hillside, gathered in the afternoon by Keble and Dicky. Our drink was always the moor water 'neat', and was known as "clear", tea or cocoa being commonly known as "thick". Bread likewise was commonly known as "dry", quite irrespective of the age of the loaf.

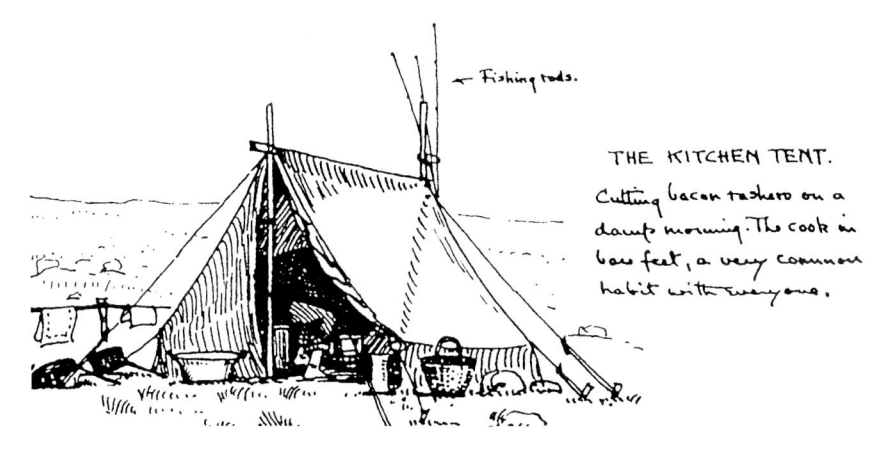

THE KITCHEN TENT.
Cutting bacon rashers on a damp morning. The cook in bare feet, a very common habit with everyone.

Jack and Edward were home late the 2nd. night running, having been fishing in the upper waters of the Avon on the other side of the Warren. Bob was also in after dark having been down to Hood in the afternoon.

It was a warm, dry, evening with a good deal of wind, and it was so delicious that we were lothe to turn in. Eventually we did so, but even then played "nap" to 12.30, when we tucked ourselves into bed. Keble said he was going to see the sun rise at 4.30. Jack said he would go fishing about the same time.

Wednesday, 1st. August.

The Chronicler awoke at 10 minutes to seven, and found a heavy wind blowing and the tent rather draughty. Keble was still asleep! Jack had disappeared however, and with Edward had gone off fishing. The perseverance of these two was truly wonderful, and so was the regularity with which they came in late for meals; on the last three days they were an hour late for lunch, an hour late for supper twice, and half an hour late for breakfast this last morning.

We were kept hard at work washing and packing all the kitchen things and packing our own bags to say nothing of doing a final shave before re-entering what is called "civilized" life.

Meanwhile rain threatened and about 11 o'clock a heavy driving mist came along, turning, about midday, into a slashing rain.

Dicky, who was lame with two sore heels, left to get down to the Parsonage by lunch time and so missed a drenching. Tucker arrived for the Champernownes goods soon after eleven, and their tent was shortly afterwards struck Ernest arrived with the Parsonage cart soon after 12.0 in the rain, and being rather before he was expected, was kept an hour waiting! We finished our packing and before striking our tent, the one last protection from the storm, we had one of the most remarkable meals of the week. A rabbit pie remains were plumped down by the pole, then followed half a loaf of bread, some cheese, half a jug of milk, and some lime juice in a bottle.

Someone volunteered to finish the milk; and the jug was filled with "clear" which, with the lime juice, made quite a good drink. But for the rabbit pie and cheese the only tool forthcoming was Arthur's pocket knife! First the cheese was cut up, then the bread, and lastly the pie into suitable pieces.....the rest was done with the fingers and front teeth.

Jack settled up with the Warrener. The tent was struck, and with Gilbert "up" our cart moved mournfully across the moor.

We were all wet to the skin by this time, and followed behind the cart talking of the past week. As we passed over the moor, Jack shouted to Gilbert "What ho! she bumps"; Gilbert was understood to say "By jove, she do!" and we picked up our bicycles and scorched home.

Meanwhile Keble had arranged to walk all the way with a view to botanizing. It was nearly 6 o'clock before he arrived at the Parsonage wetter than wet, having lost his way getting off the moor. However, he came in whistling, and brought in a large collection of weeds and things.

Provisions consumed in camp 25 July to 1 August by 7 persons.

Daily:- 5 lbs. Bread; 3½ pints milk.

In the week:
2 beef steak pies	2 rabbit pies	1 leg of mutton 11 lbs.
1 Ham (2 halves)	1 English tongue	4 lbs bacon (5 times)
5 lbs plain cake	1 lb. cheese	1½ lbs. butter (not v. good)
1 doz. hard boiled eggs	20 fresh eggs	1 lb. Devon cream

Dartmoor trout.

Groceries:
2½ large packets Quaker Oats.	½ lb. cornflower
1½ lbs. tea	2 lbs. loaf sugar
1 lb. gran. sugar (ran out)	½ lb. brown sugar
12 lbs. jam. too much alike.	2 lbs. wortleberries
Lumps of dripping	Tin of salt
Some mustard	A little pepper.

CAMP 1907

1907   PUPPER'S HILL CAMP

The Champernownes were encamped at Sherberton, with ladyfolk nearby in the farmhouse to help them with the cooking! Although the Champernownes may not have understood fully, there were several reasons why we were unwilling to forsake our old camping ground to join their party.

Their absence made the party very small at Puppers Hill, only Jack, Arthur, Keble and Walter Medlicott were found to attend the annual camp. Medlicott, you must know, is the well known London architect, and for size counts as two particularly at night in a bell tent.

Except for a deal of correspondence the first item of this year's camp was a visit paid by Jack and Arthur to Mr. Tope's Shop in Plymouth, where they purchased a second bell tent.

It had only been used for Yeomanry training and was "just as good as new". Certainly it was much superior to a second hand army tent offered to us, through which Jack happened to put two fingers by mistake just in time to save our purchasing it.

On the way to the station they spent 53 seconds in an ironmongers shop, purchasing a 10/6 "Primus" stove, which was henceforth known as "the roarer" on account of the noise emitted by the thing when burning.

They caught their train by running, and were in time to meet Medlicott's train at Totnes. The Roarer forgot to get out, however, and had to be wired for to Newton Abbott whence it safely returned.

Tuesday, 23rd. July.

Things were not so ready as usual on Tuesday morning, owing partly to the fact that Keble only reached home at 12.30 the night before. But the cart, piloted as usual by Ernest, started soon after eleven, with a rather lighter load than usual inspite of the extra tent and various bits of matchboarding and odd bits of wood for various purposes.

Medlicott and Arthur went by the 11.49 from Staverton to Buckfastleigh and walked up to the camp. The cart caught them up half way whilst having lunch, and shortly afterwards a shiny object hove in sight and was found to be Jack's bald head.

After a halt at Cross Furzes farm where we were most hospitably entertained and given a glass of cider each, we reached camp about 3.0 and, very shortly after, Ernest and the cart had disappeared over the hill on their return journey; the two tents went up, and things began to get straight.

Keble, who was still making the acquaintances of his family when we left, had promised to be up by 3.30. But wagers were offered freely about that time that he would not be up till 4.30; and he wasn't.

The weather was dull and as evening closed in we worked in a fine drizzle which soon gave the tents a well washed appearance. About 10 p.m. the moon appeared but only for five minutes.

Wednesday, 24th. July.

We slept in the old tent, the new one doing duty as kitchen and mess tent. And about 3 a.m. it was put to the test, for a heavy storm drenched everything, causing Jack to hastily tumble out and slacken all ropes.

The morning broke with a heavy driving mist enveloping everything, and so it remained the greater part of the day.

Bathing was abandoned as not worth the drenching it involved, the morning being spent in completing our equipment and keeping things dry. Jack and Medlicott, who had on arrival made the tables (one outside and one inside) and a bench, made a most useful shelf on the underside of the table for books and fishing tackle.

In the afternoon it cleared somewhat and Jack and Medlicott went off across the Warren and fished the upper waters of the Avon. Jack had success and brought in fourteen; and meanwhile Arthur added 4 more from the Warren Stream.

This year we decided that no lunch should be cooked, nor any plates used for it which saved much time and washing up, and made it quite unnecessary to come in at any special hour till we felt inclined that way.

Keble and Arthur made an excellent blancmange for supper and as soon as supper was cleared and the cocoa had been brewed we all turned in hoping for a fine morning.

Thursday, 25th. July.

The night was again quite warm owing to the S.W. wind and a wet tent, and we slept heavily. The morning was thick but not very wet though we were entirely enrapt in clouds drifting up the valley. From time to time however it rained hard and so it went on without lifting the whole day.

However, after lunch we each pocketed a goodly piece of cake and a banana for our tea, and clad in waterproofs, went out.

Jack, Arthur and Medlicott went across to the Avon and fished, Jack again having most success.

Keble went further afield. Passing over the Warren he passed the boulders on the

Avon; then steering by the wind, for nothing was visible in the mist beyond 100 yds., he passed Redlake and got into the valley of the Erme. Here he stopped to eat his tea, not knowing quite where he was; but suddenly the mist lifted and he saw his objective, the wood below Sharp Tor, a mile below him. He even saw the sun for a few minutes going to the wood, though the fog was down again all the way home past Three Barrows. He brought back his first specimen of Corydalis

Friday, 26th. July.

Friday morning was perfect, absolutely perfect. The sun shone, and soon every blanket in camp was spread out to dry, not before they wanted it.

The first event was the sending of a telegram home by Pearce to say how fine it was, and that we were expecting a party to visit us during the day. Keble soon after eleven dropped over Skerriton Down to meet the party. But even then it was turning thick and beginning to rain, and we afterwards learnt that the telegram never arrived till the afternoon.

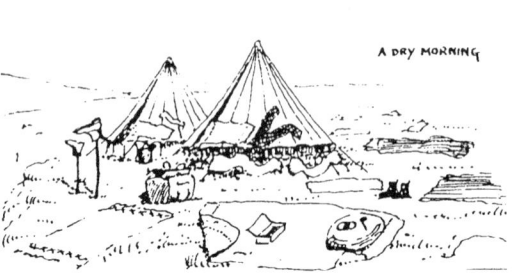

A DRY MORNING

It was fortunate no ladies came out during the day for the whole afternoon the rain descended from clouds that lay on the hills round about 100 feet above us.

Keble did not turn up again till dusk, and had it been any other member of the party we might well have been anxious as the moor was just right for losing one's way. But he arrived safely having lunched at home in the dry, although he returned to camp the wettest of any.

Jack and Medlicott went to get some rabbits. Medlicott returned, and for half an hour Jack most mysteriously disappeared. He, however, had only been stalking a rabbit which seemed to enjoy being shot at.

Arthur, who had got in about five, heard "a hollering", and found it emanated from the Warren House, where there was waiting a dripping telegraph boy with a wire to say the ladies were not coming. The fact was then fairly obvious.

Saturday, 27th. July.

The morning was dull, yet from the first it looked like a fine day. And so it turned out. The one incident of the morning was that Medlicott, who was a 'great bather' dropped the soap in the bathing pool and, inspite of all his efforts, it remained as food for the fish among the boulders at the bottom. It was a curious sight!

Keble had arranged with the party at home to meet them at Three Barrows for lunch, if fine. But one thing everyone does is to blame everyone else for being late, and on this occasion we did not get off till 12.45. Three Barrows is nearly 4½ miles away and we did not get there till two. Keble ran and was there 10 minutes before the rest.

After lunch, Dora, Mildred, Medlicott, Arthur and Keble left Agnes Champernowne and Jack on Three Barrows and visited what was known as Keble's Wood. On the way we saw Buzzards sailing overhead. The wood is a bit of a virgin forest, nearly as curious as and much more beautiful than Wistmans Wood. The Erme runs along the bottom of the wood and completes the interest from a natural history point of view.

After a few moments halt on Three Barrows after our climb from the wood below, the ladies set off in the direction of Western Beacon and we turned away into the moor on our way back to camp.

Everybody felt completely worn out on the way back but, as no one liked to own it, we went pounding along remorselessly. That evening there was a very good rabbit pie made by the Warrener's wife with rabbits shot by Jack. Arthur was seedy however and Jack was none too fit, though both were well again by next morning.

Sunday, 28th. July.

Saturday had been quite fine except for a slight drizzle on our way home; but Sunday was wet; wet in the morning and wet in the afternoon and after a couple of hours dull and fine, the evening set in wet.

Matins occured in the kitchen tent just before midday, and evensong was postponed till about 10 p.m. as the Pearces had a friend with them and were unable to have it up there.

During the two or three moderately fine hours after tea the whole camp set to work to make a causeway across the old dyke in front of camp. Medlicott, in bare feet, was constantly performing Herculean feats, not without imminent danger to himself and his assistants. Finally, ferns were rooted up from the stream, and along with foxgloves and a solitary toadstool, they were all planted to give a most naturalistic and finished "landscape gardening" effect to our work. The work did us all good and we turned in the better for it.

THE CAUSEWAY

Monday, 29th. July.

The morning was fine but rather uncertain, and there was a strong wind all day. In fact strong winds were very common all through this year's camp. The great event was to be a visit from Mr. and Mrs. Henry Medlicott who were coming up from the Parsonage with Dora and Nancy.

The morning was spent by Medlicott in deepening the bathing pool by damming the outlet with huge boulders. This he did most successfully, deepening it about 9 inches.

Our visitors arrived to find the camp in spic and span order; but unfortunately it was very stormy and came on to rain heavily about 4.0 p.m., just when tea was being prepared. The result was that eight people had tea in one bell tent, and a jolly good tea it was, with jam and cream and cakes. Our visitors had the pleasure, when they were arriving, of seeing the higher hills being steadily enveloped in the clouds, a sight which needs be seen to be appreciated, but one to which we were used.

The three ladies were rigged up in our waterproofs and, escorted by Medlicott and Jack, left about 5.15 to walk to Hayford where John and their carriage were put up.

The evening was spent by Jack and Medlicott in further deepening the bathing pool with great success.

Tuesday, 30th. July.

The night had been cooler than most but we were still in the clouds when we awoke. However the strong wind previously mentioned again sprang up and though at times threatening, we had practically no rain.

It was packing up day. Everyone was late, and told the others to hurry up. Long before things were half ready Ernest appeared on the N.E. horizon with the cart, and had about 1½ hours wait before camp was finally cleared.

Arthur and Medlicott set off walking to Buckfastleigh. Jack tried to ride his bicycle (which had been in the kitchen tent throughout camp!) and came several howlers before reaching the road. Keble took his time as usual.

Medlicott, who was appointed photographer to the brigade, took his two last snap shots of the loading up, and his photographs remain the only portion of this year's camp we now have to look forward to.

Facts and Figures - 1907

'Three Barrows' is 60 minutes walk from camp.
Sharp Tor is 75 minutes walk from camp.
Camp is 2 hrs. up from the Parsonage per bicycle.
Parsonage is 1¼ hrs. down from camp.
Camp is 2 hrs. walk from Buckfastleigh. 1hr. 45mins. back.

Suggestions for 1908

That the frying pan should not have any <u>large</u> holes in it.
That there should be a plum pudding.
That breakfast cups hold more than tea cups.
That we should borrow a quart can for carrying milk.
That we should take enough matches and cocoa, also saucepan brush and hone.

Expenses.

Cooking lamp Roarer	10.6	
Lamp	1.6	
Teapot	.10	
Methylated	.2	
Dubbin	.6	13.6
Warren for bread and milk		14.6
Subscription to S.W.Hunt		10.6
New tent		3.15.8
	Total	£5.14.2
	Divided by 3 each	£1.18.0

CAMP 1908

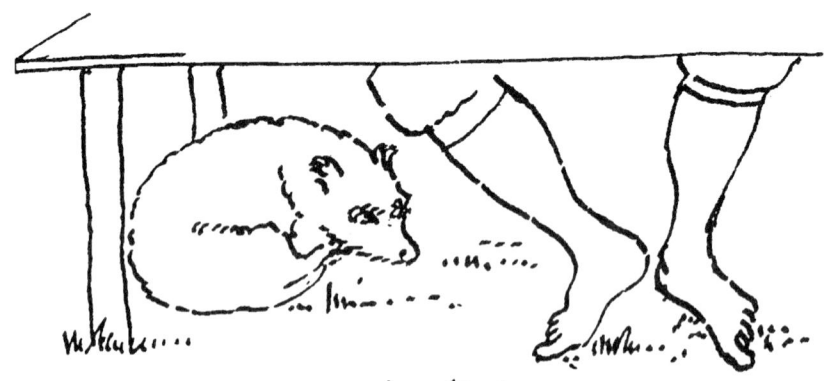

Under the table

THE DIARIES

Monday, 13th. July.

There were found six starters in the race to camp on Monday morning. Their names and weights were as follows: Jack 12 st. 1 lb., Medlicott 12 st. 1 lb., Arthur 11 st. 5 lb. Willy 10 st. 5 lb., Emile Fauguet 11 st. 10 lb., and Keble who was so late that he was not weighed. The other five, after waiting at the Parsonage till a terrific storm was over, which came clean through the dining room roof, started by the 11.49 a.m. from Staverton. After weighing themselves at Buckfastleigh and making many purchases they arrived in camp with the Parsonage cart in Ernest's charge and Longcause cart in Mark Heath's charge at 3.0 p.m. Keble arrived soon after 7.0 p.m. much like last year!

There was a most important seventh person in camp this year in the shape of a dog, Medlicott's Aberdeen terrier named Judy or more familiarly 'Buggins'. Buggins was 'great' after rabbits and took to camp life like the best of us.

In the evening Arthur and Emile went to Hayford Farm to fetch 30 lbs. of bread, most of which Emile insisted on carrying himself.

Emile loaded with 24 lbs of bread.

Tuesday, 14th. July.

We all slept well except that it was rather cold in the early morning, and about 6.50 the first man began to make himself a nuisance to the rest until he began preparing breakfast. The bathing pool was delicious and so were the bacon and eggs beautifully poached by Medlicott. It was a beautiful day but

J.S.M. stalking rabbits in front of camp.

rather cold and it was mostly spent quietly. Willy and Arthur secured a dozen fish between them and three rabbits were brought in by Jack and Willy.

We adhered to our last year's rule of having a sandwich lunch only, so that every member should be free, and so that no washing up should be necessary. During the day further benches, the outside table and a bookshelf were made by the handyman and his assistant for the greater comfort of all.

Keble went off to Ryders Hill and as it was a clear day was able to see the flagstaff on Yes Tor at 17 miles, also the Wellington Monument no less than 44 miles away. He returned triumphant with Splachum Sphericum.

So home to mutton, hot potatoes and peas, followed by an excellent hot plum pudding, not forgetting the hot cocoa before turning in.

Wednesday, 15th. July.

Up in good time after another cool night we were quite ready for our breakfast of fish and bacon. Keble and Medlicott went over to Hayford directly breakfast was finished to send letters and fetch the post, as the postman did not come over the moor except on two days in the week.

The morning began with a much needed shave all round, and an airing of tents and bedclothes, as there had been a certain amount of wet on and off. Then, pocketing luncheons, Jack and Willy went down the Avon to fish, and Medlicott and Arthur went up the Avon as far as the boulders. But the combined catch was only six trout, and all came home to tea.

We were all just in when swish came the rain with a strong south-west wind. The rain increased and with a gale blowing penetrated through where it was not wanted.

The night was very stormy and Arthur, who was sleeping on the windward side of the old tent had to shift his bed owing to the wet, and it was a boney patch he moved to.

The prospect of wet was less pleasant this year as the Pearces had left the Warren House which was inhabited by clay diggers.

Thursday, 16th. July.

Wet in the morning, wet in the afternoon and wet at night sums up Thursday. The storm moderated slightly between one and 3.0 p.m. but it hardly ever stopped raining.

The stream, and especially the Avon below, were both in flood. All the pools disappeared under a thick foaming torrent, boulders being marked by huge waves.

As usual our spirits rose with the storm - also wit was rife. A new definition was found for the word waterproof 'That which will hold no more wet'. Willy's usual remark of approval was "I say! top hole", and of disapproval "you limit". Medlicott's swear word was "Sauvida". Jack's expression of appreciation was "A1 Lloyds copper bottom". Emile's every third remark was "Oh! bovver". Another camp saying originated when Arthur, after burning himself with a hot potato, warned others "not to let go with their forks too soon".

Towards evening various members became restless. Jack followed Willy's example and went "worming", getting very wet and few fish. Keble and Emile went off to Buckfastleigh and bought various articles which were missing, getting home wet and tired about 9.0 p.m., wetter even than the postman who turned up in the morning.

For dinner we had a beautiful hot soup concocted by Medlicott and having fifteen ingredients. It was O.K.

Friday, 17th July.

We awoke to find the world just as wet as we left it and though there was some improvement, especially towards evening, we were unable to dry anything. In fact, we all got one stage wetter.

The streams were clearer but still much swollen so that fishing with the fly was impossible. The wind still blew a gale also.

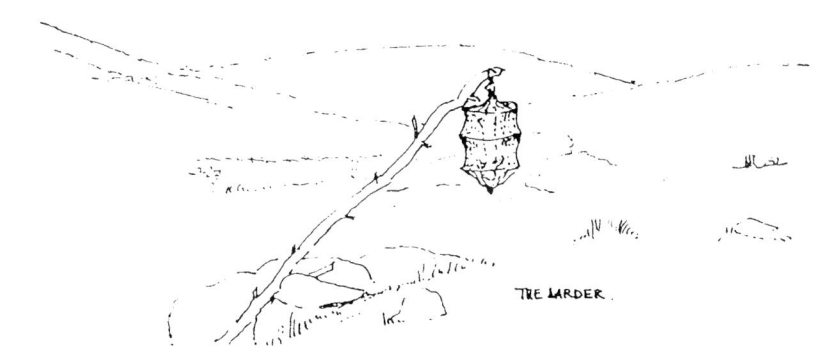

THE LARDER.

Again, owing to the wet, very little occurred till the evening when Keble went off to Brent to post letters, not returning till dark. Meanwhile, acting on the camp maxim "All gude fish come to 'uke", Willy and Jack went fishing with worms with success enough to prove the maxim true.

As usual dinner was very late not being finished till 10 p.m. partly on account of the elaborate cooking by Medlicott and his assistants and partly because fishing was possible till after 9 o'clock.

During the evening we made a noise which was partly glee singing and partly laughter. They both seemed quite good for the digestion. Jack again found it impossible to sleep in his own tent, going over to dryer quarters in the Keble, Medlicott and Willy tent.

Saturday, 18th. July.

The job that ruled the day was cricket at Dartington against Totnes, in which Jack, Arthur, Willy and Medlicott were all due to play. We were all up in good time and the four cricketers departed with Buggins about 9 o'clock. It was a dull morning, soon turning to a fresh sunny day with a good deal of wind. Keble and Emile were left behind and had a busy day, first of all drying every piece of clothing and every blanket in camp. They then turned the kitchen tent round so as to have the door away from the N.W. wind. Finally, they re-turfed the kitchen tent as during the wet the floor had become squashy and, in places, almost muddy. Then they cooked dinner, a rabbit stew, mostly made the day before by

CAMP 1908

Medlicott, and awaited the cricketer's return.

The cricket meanwhile ended in a draw, before the rank and fashion of the neighbourhood, Mr. Copleston making a brilliant 20. Dartington made 96 and Totnes made 56 for 7 wickets. The four from camp finally left the Parsonage, driving to Buckfastleigh. Thence, with a 20 minutes wait at Hayford, as Mr. and Mrs. Rew only got home a few minutes before us, they arrived dog tired (like Buggins) to supper and a pipe between 10.0 and 11.0 p.m.

Sunday, 19th. July.

After such a heavy day as Saturday everyone, except Keble, looked forward to a quiet day. The day was perfect from early morning onwards and everyone enjoyed the bathe. Keble had breakfast just before the others and started off at 8.45 to walk 8 miles to Dean Prior to take duty for Mr. Perry Keene toxophiliting in the Olympic games. Emile, at the same time went off to church at Buckfastleigh.

The others, the four cricketers of the day before, had Matins about 11.30, but otherwise did little except "mouch around", which was a term applied to the way Buggins went sloping about after the rabbits.

Keble did not return till after 4 o'clock in time for tea, and joined us in a rifle match. The target was a 4 inch tin cover on the Warren across the stream, a distance of 60 yds. about, and it was soon riddled. Then a moving target was erected with a string from the top of a tent sloping away to the moat, on which one of Medlicott's slippers was hung with a pulley wheel. After 3 shots, of which one hit, it was voted dangerous and abandoned.

Inspite of the usual attempt to get supper early, it was again well after 10 p.m. by the time we had finished. Then we sang the family hymn 595 (see Appendix 1) before having cocoa and turning in.

Monday, 21st. July.

Another fine day dull and warm early becoming bright and hot later, but turning dull again in the afternoon.

Medlicott was leaving; and almost before the breakfast was cleared Mr. Rews cart appeared over the hill. Medlicott meanwhile had reported an adder among some rocks near camp which were on the way to the bathing pool. So as soon as Medlicott and his dog had gone we had a serpent hunt but without a kill.

The day was spent by Jack, Arthur and Willy fishing and they brought in 19 nice trout. Up to Monday evening 71 trout had been caught in 7 days.

Keble and Jack went over to Hayford in the evening to meet the cart that took Medlicott to Buckfastleigh and brought back, with the milk, a hamper sent up from Dartington. Medlicott also purchased tea and other necessities in Buckfastleigh and Totnes which came in handy.

Arthur was the cook and had supper ready by 7.30, a whole hour and a half earlier than usual, with the result that we turned in at 11 p.m. instead of 12 p.m.

A pair of ravens came over camp during the afternoon.

Tuesday, 22nd July.

Arthur did not sleep well, and at 4.45 a.m. was joined by Jack outside the tent as it was a warm, fine, morning with a heavy dew. Then, in their pyjamas they started stalking a rabbit, then another and another wandering with bare feet as they were for some ¾ mile.

They returned and disturbed the others about 6.15 and breakfast occurred about 7.30.

It proved the brightest and hottest day we had had. Fishing was consequently only moderately successful, but in the evening Jack and Willy brought in some rabbits.

After tea, Keble disappeared and did not return till 9.40 having been to Brent and purchased a cake, some jam and other items. There was a very good supper awaiting him, soup, beef, potatoes, carrots and broad beans.

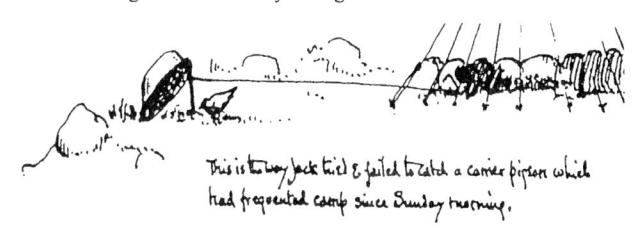

This is the way Jack tried & failed to catch a carrier pigeon which had frequented camp since Sunday morning.

Emile broke his previous record by going over to Hayford and bringing back six 4 lb. loaves, 1 lb. of butter and a gallon of milk.

It was a beautifully warm evening and except for Willy, who had a bad cold, no one even donned their sweater, the regulation camp evening dress. Keble and Jack were late turning in, but all slept soundly after a long, hot, day.

Wednesday, 23rd. July.

Though not quite so early as on Monday, camp was astir in good time as Keble had got up soon after six and had gone off to spend the last three days of his holiday at home. It was again a roasting hot day. For breakfast we had porridge, trout, bacon and poached eggs on a potato and bean mash fired and browned in the oven. Even Emile was learning to eat a good English breakfast! The morning was spent generally cleaning and preparing to let one tent and a good deal else be fetched by the cart on Thursday morning when Arthur intended to leave. Willy's cold was better, judging from his remark at 7.15 "My hat! you are a lazy lot of limits; it's a top hole morning".

We tried a new arrangement of meals. Theoretically we abolished tea as such (practically we had a very good one as we thought there was a possibility of some of the ladies visiting camp). Then we had supper soon after 7 o'clock. Next we all went fishing till dark, leaving the washing up till later. Finally we had cocoa and a general wash up about 10 o'clock, getting to bed in quite good time, but despairing of the sulky temper of the trout we failed to catch.

RESULT of FISHING on WEDNESDAY EVENING!

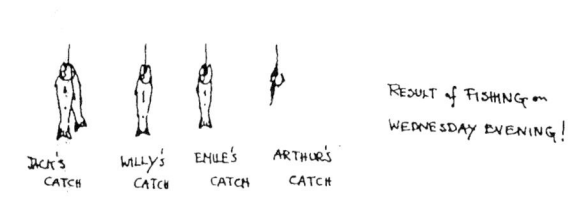

JACK'S CATCH   WILLY'S CATCH   EMILE'S CATCH   ARTHUR'S CATCH

Thursday, 23rd. July.

A beautiful, warm, sunny morning greeted us and made our bathe even more perfect than usual. Then came breakfast about 8 o'clock, cooked by Jack. We were beginning to make better use of our oven, keeping things hot in it till people were ready.

It was a morning of packing for Ernest and the cart arrived about 12.15 and took away as much as could be spared. Jack had dropped his scissors somewhere along the Avon, a mile and a half away, the evening before and on going to look for them was lucky enough to find them almost at once.

Arthur left at 1 o'clock, walking home by Dry Bridge and Rattery. Steering by his shadow, he struck moor gate exactly though it is 4 miles from camp, and a walk he had never done.

In the afternoon Jack and Emile went over to Redlake to see what the clay diggers were doing. They found a dirty hut with two idle engineers in it, also some twenty holes which filled with water as quickly as they were dug. Jack suggested to the engineers they should get a theodolite and plot the various holes on the 25" ordnance, which seemed to them a lot of trouble, but rather a good idea. To the foreman he suggested that instead of pumping from 6.30 a.m. to 3 p.m. to empty the hole before the days work, he should get a small oil engine to keep the place dry. Judging from his own description, Emile fell about in deep puddles of water and soft clay in the most dangerous fashion. Emile learnt later to skin and cut up a rabbit.

Friday, 24th. July.

Only Jack, Willy and Emile were left, with but two tents and half the crockery and cooking utensils.

Emile complained very much of the way Jack "zlumped" on him in the morning to wake him, but as he was sleeping right across the door of the tent it was not surprising.

The morning was spent packing. Ernest arrived soon after midday and shortly afterwards, some worn patches of grass, a few trenches and a milk can were the only signs of our camp. Emile went over the hill with the cart; Jack and Willy returning for an hour and a

quarter to fish, before catching the 4 o'clock train at Buckfastleigh. They caught 7 trout thus bringing up the total for 10 days to 102 fish.

"All gude fish come to 'uke".

Camp Expenditure - 1908

Baker. L Hunt. Buckfastleigh	11.4	Bread arranged 1 lb. per head per day.
Milk etc. Mr. Rew, Hayford farm	£1. 4.5	Milk arranged 1 pint per head per day
including 5 deliveries @ 1/- each		46 eggs in 60 man days.
Oil from Petherbridge. Buckf.gh.	4.0	6 gals. in 10 days.

Total cost (including 15/- hire of tent, 14/6 repairs to tent. and 11/3 new waterproofs) was £5.0.0. of which W.B.M. paid 10/- and the rest 18/- each.

The following is a list of provisions taken and consumed or partially so:-

Quaker oats	3 pkts	1 Tongue	Crockery	
Cornflower	1 pkt	1 Beefsteak pie	8 large plates	8 small plates
Tea	2¼ lb.	1 leg mutton	8 large cups	8 saucers
Loaf sugar	2 lbs	1 Ham	5 egg cups	2 T pots
Granulated sugar	3 lbs	16 hard b, eggs	9 large knives	6 small knives
Demarara	2 lbs	1 plum pudding	1 pair carvers	8 forks
Jam	8 lbs	4 lbs dough cake	2 large spoons	1 iron spoon
Marmalade	4 lbs	1 Pigeon pie	8 dessert spoons	8 tea spoons
Salt	2 lbs	1 Pressed beef	2 milk jugs	2 milk cans
Cheese	2 lbs	Vegetables	Tin opener	Table cloth-
Mustard	Pepper	Bacon 7 lbs	Platter (wood)	Dustbin &
Cocoa	Soda	Currant cake	Hardware	
Pineapple chunks	2 tins	Tools etc	Range kettle and steamer	
Dripping	Limejuice	Spade	1 tall tin kettle	
Whiskey	1 bottle	Pick	Enamd. saucepan and bowl	
Soap	1½ doz, matches	Hatchet	2 washing bowls	
candles and ends	1 box	Tool bag	Aluminium saucepan	
Condensed milk	Chocolate	Boot polish	Frying pan	
Furniture, etc.		2 looking glasses	Hanging lamp	
3 bell tents, poles and pegs		2 soap dishes	2 candle lanterns	
Table and bench boards		2 rifles and ammo.	1 saucepan brush	
3 carpet chairs		Rods etc.	3 tea cloths	
7 waterproof sheets		Gun oil	1 wash cloth	
7 prs blankets			Grease paper	
7 pillows			1 muslin meat safe	
			1 picnic case (not used)	

Note: Camp lasted 60 one man days.

CAMP 1909

Monday, June 29th.

The preparation of the various camp belongings was this year in the hands of Jack who ably supervised the packing done by Dora and Mildred.

Arthur and Medlicott arrived at Dartington on Saturday night at midnight. Willy came down on Sunday morning.

Keble, who was busy getting ready to get married and to become Vicar of Wrath, did not arrive till Tuesday.

Ernest brought round the cart at 10 a.m. being followed shortly by a second cart in charge of the young Robert Austen. The carts were quickly loaded and by 11 a.m. were on their way to pick up Jack's belongings at Meads.

Medlicott and Arthur caught the usual train 11.49 at Staverton; while Jack, who first had to attend to a double swarm of bees ably taken by the first two on Sunday morning, and Willy followed on bicycles.

The company re-assembled at Buckfastleigh and after partaking of the customary glass of cider set out for camp. The day was perfect, rather dull but very dry.

As soon as the Warren was sighted Jack and Willy went forward as a patrol to investigate a certain pony carcase reported to exist about ¼ mile above camp. This they found to be in an advanced state of decomposition, so as soon as the carts were emptied they were sent up to cover it up with earth. This entirely abated the nuisance. But there were a surprising number of carcases in different directions, which were supposed to indicate the recent hard winter.

The three tents were got straight very quickly and the various members of the party went fishing with sufficient success to provide a dish for breakfast.

Medlicott's weight proves too much for a camp stool.

In the course of cooking supper there was a loud report and Medlicott with his hands full descended to the ground, the canvas of a camp stool having snapped under his weight. "Sauvida! *that* will take some mending" was his immediate comment though it was not apparent whether he referred to the chair or himself. He, luckily, referred to the chair, so we laughed hugely.

We turned in with a dry wind blowing, a beautiful moon shining, and had a fairly good night.

Tuesday, 29th. June.

About 5.20, Arthur and Willy, in the tent behind, became restless, and Medlicott and Jack were not allowed to remain long undisturbed. It was a cold morning but the sun soon cleared off the dew, and by 7.0 a.m. when breakfast was ready it was warming the world nicely.

There seemed wonderfully few rabbits about, yet our larder soon acquired four of them. Of these one was caught by Buggins who was evidently pleased with her performance. But most of the rabbits fell to Medlicott's extremely nice rifle, a model of the service rifle.

There was considerable speculation as to whether Keble would arrive during the day and, if so, when. He did not turn up till nearly 10 p.m. carrying all his luggage over the moor from Hayford.

Meanwhile, Jack had been up to the Warren House to see what he could pick up, as it was empty and quite deserted. He came back with some rhubarb which was promptly turned to account for supper.

The wind got up in the evening and all found it rather cold, but everyone had a sweater and used it.

Wednesday, 30th. June.

A rather warmer night made us all sleep well and lie in bed rather late. Breakfast did not occur till 8.30 and a huge breakfast it was, for there were no fewer than 31 small trout to cook besides all the other things.

The early mornings were remarkable for the songs of the Meadow Pipits which were soaring and parachuting all round the camp. There were also a number of young Wheatears in the immediate neighbourhood.

During our absence from camp too, the cattle were rather a nuisance, being very inquisitive.

It was another very hot, bright, day and trout were hard to catch. Still, it had many compensations and we had breakfast, lunch and supper all out of doors.

In the evening Jack and Willy and Mendicott went fishing and Arthur and Keble went up Ryders Hill after birds. They put up Snipe and found an astonishing number of Wheatears. The Snipe were seen and heard "drumming".

The various members of the camp did not collect again till 10 p.m. late fishing and walking being made posible by a beautiful moon.

Thursday, 1st. July.

Another windy and draughty night brought another very hot day and meals again were all taken on the outside table.

Rifle shooting was a great attraction on these holidays, targets 5" x 6" made out of a cardboard box (in which Medlicott's field glasses arrived) being placed on the Warren at ranges varying from 50 to 180 yards, all of which were perforated by Medlicott's rifle.

Medlicott discovered a Wheatear's nest on the way to the bathing pool with 5 eggs, while Keble and Jack both discovered Skylark's nests with 3 eggs. But the Meadow Pipit's nests quite beat us. A great number of Rooks came up to the Warren each day to feed, and Carrion Crows and Ravens were seen frequently. Plover and Missel Thrushes were also about in large flocks.

In the evening a heavy wind blew from the N.N.W. and all the pegs and ropes had to have attention as the tents were roaring in the wind.

During the day, Jack made an excellent lamp shade out of copper wire with the help of 'Tinol' soldering apparatus. This improved the lighting of the kitchen tent very much, though it was only used from 10 to 11 p.m. each evening, during cocoa time.

For the third year medlicott tried his hand at oatmeal biscuits made out of old porridge with the inevitable addition of a pat of butter without which nothing was complete in his estimation

Friday, 2nd. July.

It looks as if we were in for the hottest and driest camp we have ever had. Again, meals were all out of doors.

Breakfast was late, and before we had washed up Mr Rew of Hayford Farm arrived with eggs and milk and cream. The last was a luxury as we expected visitors, Willy having gone down to fit his (Keble's) wedding clothes at Totnes, with instructions to bring a plenty of ladies back to tea.

Early in the morning the cattle were cured of their inquisitivness by a curious incident. One was heard sniffing near the back tent in which Arthur, Keble and Willy slept. Soon the animal's shadow fell on the tent, over Arthur's bed. Then its nose sniffed and touched the tent, a signal for a violent blow from inside delivered by Arthur from his bed. They went off like smoke and have not yet returned to find out what happened.

During the morning everyone shaved, and camp was cleaned and tidied, all tents being opened up. But it was not till 4.30 that the first of our visitors hove in sight, causing Jack and Medlicott to return with Buggins from rabbiting and Arthur from fishing.

The visitors were Aunt Louisa, Nancy, Margaret Cornish, Dora and Mildred. John and Mark, who had driven the party up, also came out to see camp and have tea.

They brought further supplies and dainties such as strawberries and a bag of shelled peas.

After inspecting camp they had a grand tea. Cups and seats were rather short but not the cream or jam. It was the largest party we had ever catered for, and we did them proud.

We had an excellent dairy this fine hot weather in the stream in which milk, cream and butter were kept and in which blancmanges and other delicacies were cooled.

The ladies left about 6.20 escorted by Jack and followed by Keble with some letters for post. Jack and Keble also brought back bread from the farm. Keble suddenly dropped his lot halfway up the hill and exclaimed "No, I have not seen that before". He had only found a new moss.

This evening we did not foregather for supper till after 8.30 owing to the disorganisation of the day. Generally we had supper between 7 and 8.0 and went out afterwards. About 8 o'clock heavy mists came rolling over Peter's cross and the Warren and tumbled down into the valleys, enveloping camp in a white and rather cold blanket. But we turned in rather early and were not much affected by it.

Saturday, 3rd. July.

The day broke cloudlessly, but we were heavy with sleep as the tents were damp, and we did not turn out till 7.30.

The morning bathe was taken in sunlight and at breakfast time it was still fine though dull and coldish, so we had it indoors.

After breakfast Mr Rew arrived with milk and almost simultaneously a "scud" whisped up the valley from the S.West and we started on a wet drizzling foggy morning. Jack and Willy went off to the Avon with fishing tackle. Medlicott and Buggins went rabitting.

Arthur and Keble remained in camp and at lunch were the only two moderately dry. Medlicott had returned with a nice rabbit caught in the old walls below the Warren House. These walls suffered considerably during the week at his hands (and Buggin's paws) as they housed many rabbits, and many stones had to be pulled away to get at them.

Jack, Arthur and Willy all caught some good fish inspite of the wet. And they brought the total catch up to 102 in the first five days of camp.

But the day remained wet, the clouds sweeping up the valley and drenching everything; but we were quite hardened to it by former years and almost enjoying it.

Jack left about 6.0 p.m. for Meads as he had to take duty all day Sunday. We learnt afterwards that he lost his way in the mist before he got to Hayford.

After dark, it stopped raining though the sky did not clear and we turned in with the tents wringing wet.

THE CHURCH

Sunday, 4th. July.

The morning broke quite dry and sunny. The bathe was quite perfect but breakfast was rather late. We did very little except mouch around looking for Wheatears nests or Meadow Pipit's nests, and watch the various farmers and shepherds out after their stock. The latter seems to be the regular Sunday morning occupation and each man was mounted and followed by a dog. Judging too from the enormously protracted conversations held when two of them met, time was no consideration.

We had Matins in a dell of rocks and ferns on the way to the bathing pool. And it was on the spot where we had just had Matins that we laid the foundations of our church. The church consisted of a rough paving on the floor of the dell, then a flight of three solid granite steps with flanking boulders up to a small grass terrace and a granite pier with a cross on it, cut in the granite by Arthur with Jack's cold chisel and hammer. (see Appendix 3).

After lunch Keble went off across the moor to preach for Jack at Brooking. He took longer than he anticipated and had no time for tea before the service. They had tea however after church and returned to camp about 10 o'clock.

The record of the 1909 camp ends here. As a matter of fact, Medlicott left early catching the 8.0 a.m. train at Buckfastleigh. The view was beautiful over Newton Abbot and Torquay as he and Arthur topped the hill above Hayford. Arthur and Jack fished down stream about 2 miles and then walked home late in the afternoon. Willy, who had been left waiting for the carts with the tents all packed, paid Mr. Rew and cycled home.

The following day Arthur and Keble went to London. Keble was married on the Thursday, Arthur being his best man.

CAMP 1910

Monday, 25th. July.

Camp was a problem. No one seemed to be able to manage it at the same time as anyone else. Besides, the Parsonage days were over, and everything dated from Longcause.

Still, Willy with the help of the log book got things into shape, and Aunt Caroline found all supplies. On Monday morning Arthur, Keble and Willy started with one 'wain', two horses, Mark Heath and Robert Clear.

Jack could not get away till August, but Medlicott was provided (and hoped) for on Wednesday morning.

Sunday had been the wettest day of the year, a continuous sou'wester. The papers on Monday morning prophesised the weather as "Stormy, some rain, wind strong, a gale in places, very cool, fine later".

It described the day exactly. We started in rain, we arrived in a gale, and the sun broke through about 5 o'clock though the wind was still boisterous.

As there were only three of us to get the tents up and our goods unpacked we all had to work hard.

Our old friend, Mr. Rew, was unable to supply us with milk since, owing to the death of his wife a few weeks before, he kept no dairy at Hayford. Keble had interviewed Mr. Common at Cross Furzes, but though willing to supply us, they had not a drop of milk at the moment. So we had our tea without milk; and in the evening Arthur and Keble called on Mr. and Mrs. Willcocks, the new tenants at the Warren House.

LONGCAUSE PORCH LOADED at 9.30 a.m.

There were eight people living in the house and only one cow, but the one cow volunteered to supply us with at least a gallon a day.

We also found we had to get leave from Lawyer Cottier, 8 Frankfurt Street, Plymouth who controlled the Warren waters under the Duchy. Our camp is on Ld. Churchill's ground, the boundary between the two being the stream.

Meanwhile, Willy had straightened the tents and it was soon time to cook the potatoes and broad beans for supper. After the usual cocoa, we turned in. It was very draughty and the ground was hard.

Tuesday, 26th. July

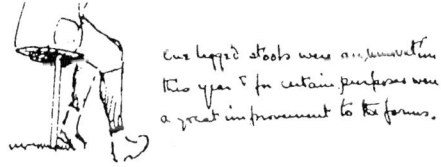

The sun shone early. It was a beautiful day, but the wind still hummed round the tents. The chief fact about breakfast was the absence of fish, to rectify which Willy went out about 10.30 and caught 7, four more being added later in the day. Score for the day; Willy 10, Arthur 1.

Keble failed us! He was asked how many legs a slug 3" long had. But he gave no plain, straightforward, answer.

The postman arrived at 11 o'clock and a letter was posted to Cottier. Keble offered to take other letters to the post after lunch and to go from Cornwood into Plymouth to see Cottier, but he didn't get very far and returned in time for tea.

Removing a large boulder from the bottom of the bathing pool.

There were a pair of Kestrels constantly hovering near the camp throughout the day. Flocks of Missel Thrushes and Starlings were seen, also Meadow Pipits, Wheatears and Grey Wagtail. One Wagtail was feeding young birds in the old wheel house below us, but we could not find the nest owing to the ruin being deep in water.

Supper was late as everyone was out and supposed the others were in. We had not finished till 10 p.m.

The night was dark with much cloud about, and before we turned in there was a suspicion of rain.

Wednesday, 27th. July.

The night was fairly still. There was a gentle, warm, S.W. wind which brought up a thick mist, developing occasionally into rain. We slept soundly and found a wet world when we awoke.

After an early cup of tea, Arthur dropped over to Hayford to meet Medlicott. Medlicott, however, came up through the farm and Arthur got back to camp after waiting 3 hrs. in vain. Medlicott had arrived at Totnes at 6.6 a.m. and got to Hayford, by trap, at 7.50.

There was a good breakfast for both of them when they came in. Buggins, who came with Medlicott, at once settled down into camp life, promptly going off to see about the rabbits and then settling down into her old place under the table.

As the morning wore on the mist lifted, and the question arose as to whether the ladies would turn up. We shaved on the off chance and Keble went to Hayford.

About 1 o'clock Keble returned with Violet; and Mark came along a few minutes later with a few vegetables, etc. Violet stayed to lunch and after going over to the boulders on the Upper Avon, had tea, leaving about 5.0 p.m.

At lunch a whole horde of men was seen approaching from the east. Bug at once gave tongue. It was an unwarranted intrusion and neither she nor anyone else approved. Keble and Arthur went out and talked to the leaders, and found it was a walking party from Christchurch, Westminster Bridge Road. Keble asked them where they thought they were going, and the leader answered "Well, we have got here."

However after a short scientific discussion about the origin of Dartmoor, they were directed to Hayford, and so to Buckfastleigh.

THE INVASION of 1910.

Medlicott, during the afternoon, found a Snipe's nest with four eggs. Also in the evening a Meadow Pipit's nest was found close to the tents with an almost full grown young Cuckoo in it, which resented discovery by violently pecking Arthur's finger. Three Ravens passed over about 6.0. Also a very large Hawk with pointed wings sailed overhead at a great height and it was suggested it might be an Osprey.

About 6.30 the evening turned wet and became wetter and wetter.

Thursday, 28th. July.

The night was a fair drencher. Yet with careful placing of the beds and attention to the tent, we all slept soundly, and dreamt of places where it wasn't raining.

The morning was thick and almost raining. But all enjoyed first a bathe, then a jolly good breakfast.

It cleared during the morning and there was a good deal of bustling about to get ready for the postman about 11.0. Willy went fishing with considerable success, Arthur with small success. Medlicott and Buggins caught a couple of rabbits.

But Lunch was made a rather punctual 1 o'clock by a heavy storm of rain which drove people in.

Medlicott and Willy started about 2.15 to Forder farm to fetch bread and cups and saucers. (The only things broken on the upward journey were 2 cups which left us with three only). But they had hardly got over the hill when down came the rain and the afternoon was as wet a one as we remember.

SLEWING the TENT 60° to get the door out of the wind.

Arthur and Keble moved the kitchen tent round so that the door might be out of the wind, and got tea ready. About 5.30 Willy and Medlicott arrived with the bread and cups. They were absolutely wet through, and had lost their way. Medlicott was sure they were down by the Avon, Willy didn't know where they were, but luckily they struck the top of the Warren Stream about a mile above camp.

The evening was simply drenching from the S.E. and was largely spent in trenching the ground around the tents to drain off the water. Each tent had a pool of water in it, and we went barefooted and barelegged in waterproofs and sou'westers.

We had a good mutton stew, and turned in tired out. The sleeping tent was terribly wet, the more violent storms causing a lot of dripping. But we went to sleep soundly inspite of it all.

Friday, 29th. July.

A beautiful morning greeted us. Our first move was at 5.0 a.m., but we thought better of it and turned in again till 7.0 a.m. The wind which had shown signs of getting round again to S.W. was now just a bit N. of west.

There was a good breeze with alternate sunshine and shade - a few slight showers did no harm.

The young cuckoo which left its nest on the 28th. was discovered in the church, still being fed by the Pipits.

Fish were rising nicely and Willy, Mendicott and Arthur all caught some. Willy caught 30, a record for camp so far.

About 9.30 a youth was observed running across the moor towards us. Presumably he had been running all the way from Buckfastleigh, for he brought an express letter and all the ordinary post. He was given an extra breakfast while we all wrote letters, postcards and telegrams.

This is where Arthur's diary keeping ends. The remainder appears to be the work of Willy.

As it was Keble and Arthur's last evening in camp, the menu for dinner was somewhat elaborate. There was clear soup, ham and chicken pie, baked marrow and potatoes, followed by plum pudding. Keble, before supper, had collected a number of plants and ferns to take back to Wath and just at supper time was seen struggling home under a large portion of Mother bog.

After the usual cup of cocoa all round, we turned in early, as the Warrener's cart was to start at 6 a.m. with the luggage.

Saturday, 30th. July.

Arthur woke first and soon after Willy had the porridge cooking on the 'roarer'. The cart arrived punctually at 6 a.m. and, after being loaded up, started across the moor for Buckfastleigh. Arthur and Keble had a hearty breakfast off porridge, ham and boiled eggs. Arthur started on ahead and was just disappearing over the top of the hill as Keble started, running, to catch him up.

After breakfast Medlicott and Willy, who were now the only two left, brailed the tents up and got all the bedding outside. About 12 o'clock the Warrener returned bringing 2 gallons of oil and a dozen eggs. The postman arrived while we were skinning rabbits; among the others there was a letter from Mr. A. E. Barrington of Tor Royal, Princetown, giving us leave to fish in the Duchy waters till Aug. 6th.

Some inquisitive cows were a great nuisance during lunch and Willy chased them off with considerable success with a mallet and a fire iron.

Nine fish were caught before lunch with a fly and presented to the Warrener and his sons who had been watching the performance. Eight more caught during the afternoon brought the total for the week (or rather for five days) up to 96.

After tea Medlicott and Willy went out to pick some wurts and Willy suddenly came upon a large snake which he killed by dropping a heavy stone on to it; it was exactly two feet long and is buried twelve yards due east of the outside table, the tomb being marked by a conical stone - this will enable the skeleton to be dug up next year.

It is found that one-legged stools, inverted, make excellent high candlesticks.

It was a beautiful still evening and for the first time since the start the canvas of the tents ceased to flap.

Supper was quite experimental. Medlicott surpassed himself by producing batter pudding and stewed wurts. Willy mashed some potatoes and fried them to a lovely 'brown' in butter and they were A1 with the ham.

After cocoa, made without milk for a change, we turned in and decided to have a long night.

Sunday, 31st. July.

We did have a long night; 8 or 9 hours unbroken sleep and after breakfast, off ham and poached eggs, we began to build the back wall of the church. There is a bog at the back of it and Medlicott suggested it would serve as a total immersion font.

About lunch time we saw, on the warren just across the stream, a rabbit chasing a stoat. The Warreners son told us that the stoat generally kills rabbits in the holes or in some confined area and cannot, like the weasel, tackle its prey in the open.

After lunch of cold rabbit stew and cold batter pudding and wurts we walked down by the Avon and for a long time watched a beautiful Sandpiper feeding among the rocks.

We saw several shepherds in the course of the day and had a visit from one who came from Combstone Tor, near Dartmeet and who talked freely of the Mallocks. Herding sheep etc. seems to be quite a feature of Sundays.

With the exception of one or two heavy showers the day was lovely, alternate patches of sunlight and shadow chasing each other down the slopes of Kratta.

Medlicott made another experiment at supper, turning out cornflower fritters flavoured with marmalade; they were a masterpiece of cooking.

We turned in early as Medlicott had to start at 7.30 a.m. to catch the 9.36 at Buckfastleigh.

Monday, 1st. August.

Willy and Medlicott rose at 6.45 and breakfast was soon ready. The Warreners cart arrived, taking Medlicott's luggage to Buckfastleigh. It was a 'topping' morning and Willy got everything out and thoroughly dried.

Calvert arrived at lunchtime, having driven up from Buckfastleigh. The afternoon turned wet at 4.30 just in time to wet Jack through as he walked up carrying a few necessaries wrapped in a towel. The rain it rained and we were content to remain in the tent, as to put a nose outside was to get it wet. By the time we turned in at 10 p.m. the rain had changed to a driving fog. Calvert could not understand why he was so sleepy, but as he had arrived at Totnes at 4.30 a.m. and had walked about till 7.45 when he presented himself at Longcause, it was excused.

Tuesday, 2nd. August.

The rain and wind had lasted all night and as the morning was not very inviting, we did not make a move until after 8 a.m. Willy turned out first and soon had a wonderful breakfast of porridge, trout and scrambled eggs. After washing up deliberately and writing some letters for post, we were glad to see the weather improving. Before lunch Calvert lost a golf ball and Willy and Jack hooked a good number of fish. Dick Wigan also took advantage of the improvement in the weather to come up from Longcause, arriving about 4 p.m.

There was no opportunity for drying anything much, since heavy showers came at intervals. Willy and Dick walked back to Hayford, Willy looking after the latters luggage, and meanwhile, Jack and Jill (Calvert) went up the hill to fetch a pail of milk and also took an offering of 20 trout. When night came there were heavy clouds rushing across the sky and looking threatening, but no rain was falling, and the tents to our joy were actually dry. The fish score for the day was 32 and this brought the total to 133.

Wednesday, 3rd, August.

Willy again apparently mistook the hour in the morning and was about soon after 6 a.m. under the impression that it was 7 a.m. However, by the time the rest of the party turned out, a sumptuous breakfast was steaming on the hob. The stream had again assumed a more normal appearance and the morning was just good enough to make bathing attractive. Unfortunately, the soap and soap dish were left at the pool, as apparently the stream was falling. But soon after breakfast the rain came again and rained as if it wanted to catch a train and by lunchtime the party was a good deal wetter than was pleasant, and the stream rushing down as hard as we have ever seen it.

Meanwhile, Jill had lost the last remaining golf ball, and his hair had got quite beyond control. Willy caught 19 trout, chiefly with flies before the flood came down and with a contribution by Dick and Jack the total reached 161.

The afternoon was showery, and Willy and Jill went to the "boulders" and saw a fine sight with the torrents coming down. As the rain came on again at 10 p.m. Willy remembered he had left two pairs of boots out to drain and left the tents to go and hunt the slipper in the darkness.

Owing to the advanced condition of the remains of the ham, it was deemed advisable to have high tea the following day. A little target practice with the rifles was indulged in between showers and for want of anything better Jill shifted a good deal of the moor with his 'iron'.

THE DIARIES

Thursday, 4th. August.

We breakfasted off porridge and 27 trout. Agnes Champernowne and Miss Hawkins of Hayford arrived about 11.30. Dick and Calvert had started rather late to meet them, which they did on Puppers Hill, just out of sight of camp.

On their way towards camp, Calvert killed a snake which, he declared, stood on its tail and hissed at them. Apparently, at the first shot at it with his stick he missed it altogether but the second sent it flying backwards over his head.

Willy went out to try and get some fish for the visitor's lunch but, though he caught half a dozen, he did not arrive back in time for them to be cooked; instead of having them at lunch therefore the ladies had to put up with them for tea.

The afternoon being rather showery, the ladies spent most of the time in the kitchen tent. At 6 p.m. Willy escorted them over the hill to Hayford.

A little rifle shooting was done in the evening; the Warrener tried his hand with a rook rifle but did not succeed in defacing the target.

We were now only three in camp as Jack unfortunately had to leave us on account of Mr. David's funeral being on Saturday and Mr. Cox not being at home to make arrangements. Turning in seemed to be quite a problem as, curiously enough, Jack's absence seemed to make less room than ever in the tent.

Friday, 5th. August.

As there were no fish, we breakfasted off porridge and buttered eggs - 15 of them. Willy decided to go down to Dartington to arrange about the cart coming up Monday instead of Saturday, as Mark Heath would be unable to come on Saturday with it. He arrived back in camp at 6.45 having walked out from Brent, up the Avon, carrying a loaf of bread. Meanwhile, Dick and Calvert had had a walk over Kratta and White Barrows.

The round of beef had to be buried in the evening before supper, so we fetched out the pressed beef which Calvert had brought up the previous Monday only to find that it was clamouring to go too. Supper seemed to take a long time and when we turned in after washing up it was not far off midnight.

Saturday, 6th. August.

Breakfast was naturally rather late and again as there were no fish, we had to resort to eggs.

It was a magnificent day and Calvert started off to Brent to post a letter. Willy was preparing to go out fishing when he found the top of his rod had been bitten off by a cow. The sun was shining on a very clear stream and the wind too was down stream on the Avon, so the catch totalled 3 for the day. Dick had 28 'rises' but they were not converted so we presumed the fish must have been rising short. Dick bathed in the Avon on the way back but having no towel, dried himself on his vest. Calvert returned about 6.30 having had a glorious walk.

We had supper off tongue and potato chips fried in dripping, which proved a great success.

The night was inclined to be wet but no great quantity of rain fell. Again, we were very late in turning in.

Sunday, 7th. August.

The visitors decided that Willy should take no part in the preparation for breakfast; they should get it all ready themselves; and they did, with the result that we had rather a late brunch at noon off poached eggs and bacon.

In the afternoon we strolled up to Ryders Hill and had a magnificent panoramic view of the moor from Princetown to Rippon Tor. The coast however was cloudy. With glasses we could see the flagstaff on Yes Tor over Cut Hill.

On our return to camp we found two people by the Warren stream - a lady and a gentleman, whose names we did not quite make out but suppose them to be a Mr. and Mrs. Cook, the latter of Buckfastleigh. The man came up and asked us if the stream was drinkable and so we asked them to tea, which they appreciated very much. After consulting the map they started for Buckfastleigh leaving Hayford on the left.

After their departure we placed several tins across the Warren stream and fairly perforated them with Rook rifles at a range of about 80 yards; one tin in particular was split down the side and altogether assumed a most shattered condition.

After an early supper off tongue, fried potato chips and cocoa, we turned in hoping to wake early as Dick was to have breakfast at 5.45 to catch an early train at Brent.

Monday, 8th. August.

At about 4.45 Calvert looked at his watch and then picked up a boot and hurled it at Dick, with singularly little effect. Willy was awake shortly after and turned out immediately to get Dick his breakfast. The porridge was ready at 5.45; the Warrener was ready with his cart at 6.10 but both porridge and Warrener had to wait for Dick. He started off in very good time, however, with the cart at about 6.30 and, as we heard afterwards, he had plenty of time to spare at Brent station.

Calvert and Willy had their breakfast after Dick had started and soon got the things washed up, as the great business of packing up had to be faced.

They worked hard till 1.30 with the result that the packing up was almost finished when the cart hove in sight. Mark Heath and Robert Austin helped with the packing up of the sleeping tent. Willy and Calvert had a sandwich lunch down by the stream and shortly after started for Buckfastleigh to catch the 4.51.

They arrived at Longcause, just after the cart, in heavy rain.

The End

Note: These camps continued in future years and the last one finished on 30th. June 1913.

BIBLIOGRAPHY

Blackburne, H. W. & Waring, H. A.
The Chapel of The Royal Military College, Sandhurst (1922)

Burnett, David, *A Royal Duchy* (The Dovecote Press 1996.)

Martin, Arthur C., *The Small House, Its Architecture & Surroundings* (Alston Rivers 1909)

Martin, W. Keble, *Over The Hills* (The Country Book Club 1969)

Martin, W. Keble, *A History of the Ancient Parish of Wath-upon-Dearne* (W. E. Farthing 1920)

Martin, W. Keble, *The Concise British Flora in Colour* (Michael Joseph 1965)

Martin, W. Keble, *Sketches for the Flora* (Michael Joseph 1972)

Moberly, C. A. E. *Dulce Domum* (John Murray 1911)

Pevsner, N. and Cherry B., *The Buildings of England: Devon* (Penguin 1989)

INDEX

Agrostis alba 22
Ashbourne 24, 30
Asplenium septentrionale 75
Beeston 30
Birds 10, 23, 24, 27, 30
Boer War 29, 35
Bovey Tracey 30
Brighstone 6
Carex pseudo-cyperus 46
Champernownes 7, 14, 19
Christ Church College, Oxford 28, 29
Coffinswell 34, 44, 46, 48, 57, 58
Combe-in-Teignhead 61, 63, 64, 76, 77
Concise British Flora in Colour 29 et seq, **Plate 8**
Cuddesdon Theological College 13, 29, 30
Dartington Parsonage 11, **12**, 13, **14**, 16, 28, 92
Dartmoor 19, **20**, **21**, 23, 24, **Plate 2**
Devonshire Association 24, 48
Duchy of Cornwall 24, 44, **45**
Duke of Edinburgh 81, 83, 84, 85
Dulce Domum 6, 7
Earl of Devon 57, 58

Exeter University 86
Exton 79, 81, 86
Flora of Devon 48, 75, 76, 82, 83
Gidleigh 77, 79
Great Torrington 63, 75
Guisborough Hall 25, 26, **Plate 3**
Haccombe 34, 46, 58
Hyloconimum squarrosum 22
International Botanical Congress 81
Keble John 6, 7
Lepidoptera 82
Lewis Carroll 29, 42
Lewis Flora 81, 84
Linnean Society 47, 48, 76, 82
Listera cordata 82
Lyme Regis 11
Marlborough 11, 42, 82
Martin Arthur C **17**, **18**, **38**, 78, **88**, **89**
Martin Audrey 27, 42
Martin Charles **5**, 7, **8**, 9, 10, 13, 16, **17**, **18**, 24, 28
Martin Charlie 8, 12, 13, **18**
Martin Dick 8, 9, 13, 14, **17**, **18**, 67, 68, 79
Martin Dora 5, 6, 7, **8**, 9, 10, 12, 18
Martin Dora (daughter) 8, 10, 12, 13, 16, **17**, **18**, 30

INDEX

Martin Edith **8**, 12, **16**, **18**
Martin family 5, 6, 7, **8**, **9**, 10, 12, 13, 16, **17**, **18**, 78
Martin George 7
Martin Jack 8, 10, 13, **18**, 19, 46, 58
Martin Katherine (Mollie) 9, 13, 16, **17**, **18**
Martin Lisette 34, 46, 76, 84
Martin Margaret (Nellie) 8, 13
Martin Patrick 31, 81
Martin Violet 24, 30, **76**, 77, 79
Martin W Keble **18**, **78**, **87**, **Plate 9**
Martin William 7
Martin's Bank 7
Moberley Edward 10, 13
Moberley George 5, 6, 7, 9, 10
Natural History Museum 30, 75, 77, 81, 83
Over The Hills 11 *et seq*
Oxford Movement 6
Post Office stamps 86, **Plate 10**
Potentilla tormentilla 22
Poulshot 9, 10, 11, 13, 16

Royal Academy 25, 27, 36
Royal Botanic Gardens, Kew 81
Royal Memorial Chapel, Sandhurst 37, **38**, **Plate 4**, 5
Salisbury 6, 9, 10
Saxifragia cernua 48
Sketches for the Flora **47**, 92
South Wraxall Manor 25
St Luke's, Camberwell 73 *et seq* **74** **Plate 7**
St Luke's, Milber 57 *et seq*, **60**, **62**, **65**, **66**, **Plate 6**
St Mary's, Dartington 14, **15**
St Olave's, Mitcham 63, 69 *et seq* 72
Swanton Novers 9
Thalictrum alpinum 48
The Small House 17, 26, 27, **27**
Wath upon Dearne 24, 31, **32**, **33**
Winchester 5, 6, 11, 25
Wood Norton 9, **9**, **Plate 1**
Woodbury 79, 81, 85, 87, **91**, 92
Wordsworth Bishop John 11

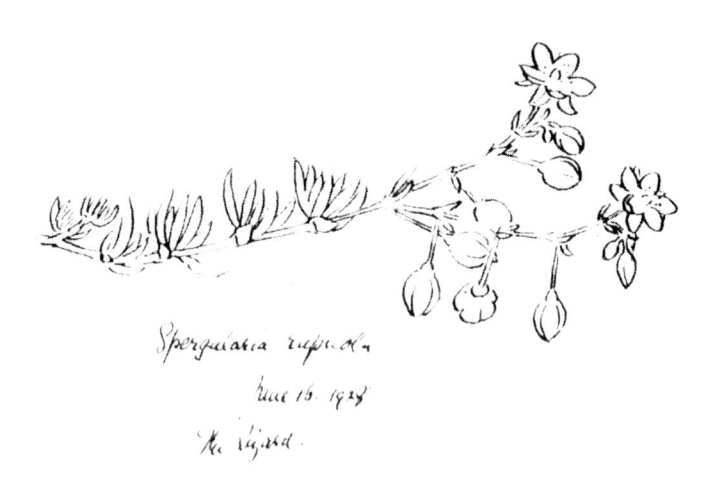

Spergularia rupicola Lebel ex Le Jolis
Rock Spurrey

Some of Keble's original sketches for the Flora
(by permission of the Linnean Society of London)